ADAM HA

Author of *24 Hours That Changed the Wor*

HALF
TRUTHS

GOD HELPS THOSE WHO HELP THEMSELVES
AND OTHER THINGS THE BIBLE DOESN'T SAY

Youth Leader Guide
by Mike Poteet

Consists of Leader Helps + Youth Study Book

Abingdon Press / Nashville

HALF TRUTHS
Youth Leader Guide

Copyright © 2016 by Abingdon Press
All rights reserved.

This book is printed on elemental chlorine-free paper.

ISBN 978-1-5018-1400-6

16 17 18 19 20 21 22 23 24 25 —10 9 8 7 6 5 4 3 2 1
MANUFACTURED IN THE UNITED STATES OF AMERICA

CONTENTS

LEADER HELPS

TO THE LEADER

Welcome to the Youth Leader Guide for the *Half Truths* study program.

The study program is based on Adam Hamilton's book *Half Truths: God Helps Those Who Help Themselves and Other Things the Bible Doesn't Say*. The book examines five commonly used sayings that sound biblical but in fact aren't in the Bible and sometimes actually work against the core messages found in Scripture. Hamilton calls these sayings *half truths*, because in most cases they get the truth partly right and partly wrong.

Half truths are a topic that youth, often passionate about honesty, will be keenly interested in. This youth component of Hamilton's study, consisting of five sessions, may be used as part of an all-ages, congregation-wide study of half truths, or by itself as a unit in your Sunday school or youth ministry programming. You can use all five sessions or a selection or a single session—although some sessions reference others, they do not build on each other in a strict sequence.

About This Youth Leader Guide

As you may have noticed on the title page and in the contents, the Youth Leader Guide consists of two parts: Leader Helps and Youth Study Book.

This first part of this guide, Leader Helps, gives you as leader the information and support you'll need to facilitate a successful study with your group. It contains session plans for the five chapters in the youth study.

The second part of the guide, Youth Study Book, reproduces in full the youth participant book, allowing you—literally—to be on the same page as your group.

Each session uses the following format:

Gather Around God's Word

Design a worship space for your group and meet there to read and pray aloud the brief litany at the beginning of each session. The Scripture responses at the beginning and end do not change from session to session, but the prayer does. You may wish to listen to joys and concerns from participants and pray about those before using the printed text as a concluding prayer. Each session includes a suggested hymn for participants to sing (or read aloud) together.

Getting Started

Each session includes an icebreaker or other activity to engage youth with the theme underlying the half truth to be discussed.

Study the Scripture

Use these questions to discuss each session's key Scripture passage. With the exception of Session 4, the Scripture passages are the same ones chosen by Adam Hamilton in *Half Truths*. Session 4 substitutes a passage Hamilton discusses at some length in the book and which should help youth get more directly to that session's content.

Read and Reflect

You may want to ask youth to read these essays on their own before your session; or, if time allows, you can have them read the essays during your meeting. Each essay examines the theology and Scripture (or lack of Scripture) behind the half truth. These Leader Helps contain questions keyed to each essay.

Suggested Activities

Each session presents four activity options intended to reinforce the content or to move youth to practical action based on the session. One of each session's activities is movie-related. (As noted, however, exercise judgment before deciding to show the clip from *Dead Man Walking* in Session 5.) If you are meeting in a setting that is not a private home, be certain your congregation participates in a program that provides a license to show film clips publicly.

Daily Bible Readings

Encourage youth to follow these six-day schedules of readings in between sessions.

Session 1

EVERYTHING HAPPENS FOR A REASON

Gather Around God's Word

This week's suggested hymn, "Be Still, My Soul," addresses in verse 2 some themes relevant to the session. Without claiming that "everything happens for a reason," the hymn text promises that God will "guide the future, as in ages past," and looks forward with hope to the day when "all now mysterious shall be bright at last." (You can find historical information about this hymn at http://www.umcdiscipleship .org/resources/history-of-hymns-be-still-my-soul.)

Getting Started

Allow youth time to complete the activity in the Youth Study Book, perhaps working in pairs or small teams. Create a collage to display for others in the congregation to see by compiling everyone's chosen headlines on a single piece of posterboard or other large sheets of paper.

Alternative: Obtain a large set or multiple sets of dominoes. Challenge youth to design, set up, and knock down a falling domino course. (Consider filming the dominoes as they fall and posting the footage to your youth group's or congregation's website.) Alternatively, obtain a *Mouse Trap* board game set, and time youth to see how quickly they can set up the trap. Ask:

- How are the things that happen to us like and unlike a chain of falling dominoes [or a game of *Mouse Trap*]?

Study the Scripture

Consider recruiting an adult from your congregation who enjoys performing to visit your group dressed as Moses and deliver **Deuteronomy 30:11-20** as a dramatic monologue.

Read and Reflect

Read or review each section of the essay, using some or all of the questions and activities below:

Do We Choose Our Own Adventures?

- Obtain a *Choose Your Own Adventure* book and read aloud from it to students for 5-10 minutes, taking group votes whenever the story calls for a decision. Majority rules! (And you can be the tiebreaker.)
- Challenge youth to rewrite a familiar Bible story in the *Choose Your Own Adventure* format.
- The essay mentions that "none of us have completely blank pages handed to us at birth." What factors determine, to some degree or another, how free we are to make choices about our own lives?

What This Half Truth Gets Right:
God Cares and God Rules

- What are some ways you have heard Christians attempt to defend God's goodness and power in the face of human suffering? How persuasive or unpersuasive do you find these *theodicies*?
- How have you experienced God's *providence* in your own life?

What This Half Truth Gets Wrong:
It Can Paralyze Us and Hurt Others

- When has someone tried to micromanage you? How did it make you feel? How did you respond?
- What other choices we make, as individuals or as a society, would cease to really matter if "everything happens for a reason"?
- What are some examples of situations in which saying this half truth might hurt someone else?

Really Choosing God

- Talk about a time when you made a choice that lined up with God's priorities and values. What happened?
- What are some things you think God has made "work together for good" in your life? Do you think God caused or used those things? Why?

Suggested Activities

1. It's a Good Thing/Bad Thing

Recruit players who are comfortable being silly in front of others; don't force any reluctant youth to play. Be ready to suggest some outlandish starting situations, if needed. Do not start with actual or realistic events, so as to avoid offending or upsetting anyone.

2. Watch a Movie

You could schedule a time for your whole group to meet and view *Signs*, or you could show the scene identified in the essay; it occurs at 0:41:10–0:45:05. Discuss using the questions in the Youth Study Book, as well as this additional question: In this conversation in the film, Graham implies that the truth of one's beliefs may not matter so long as they bring comfort. What do you think about this opinion?

3. Plot a Personal Timeline

Reassure youth that they need not share their timelines with anyone else unless they wish to do so.

4. Make a Mobile

If needed, step-by-step instructions and templates for mobiles are readily available online at craft sites such as these: http://www.pedagogyideas.com/1517/making-mobiles-clothes-hanger-mobile/ (which is very close to the mobile described in the Youth Study Book) or http://www.artistshelpingchildren.org/mobilesartscraftsideaskids.html (which calls for multiple wire hangers). If possible, arrange for your group's mobiles to be displayed for others in the congregation to see.

Daily Bible Readings

Encourage youth to follow these six-day schedules of readings in between sessions.

Session 2

GOD HELPS THOSE
WHO HELP THEMSELVES

Gather Around God's Word

This week's suggested hymn, "Grace Alone," develops the dual nature of God's grace. The first verse emphasizes God's grace as God's help for the helpless; the second verse highlights how God's grace moves us to help others.

Getting Started

Allow individual students time to attempt the activities described in the Youth Study Book. If they can't do the activities, the students are doing them correctly! If some youth have physical limitations preventing them from trying either activity, create alternate, minor experiences of "helplessness" for everyone (for example, put together a jigsaw puzzle without looking at the sides of the pieces that have the pictures; sing the alphabet song in five seconds).

In addition, or as an alternative to the printed activity, have youth run a relay race that involves teammates helping each other. For example, form two teams and give each team an inflated balloon. Team members run the race two at a time, moving the balloon to the finish line and back while keeping it continually in the air, batting it back and forth between them. If the balloon drops, neither racer may pick it up but must wait for a third teammate to pick up the balloon and return it to them. (For added difficulty, the pair of players must then start over again, instead of resuming the race from where they dropped the balloon.) After the race, ask:

- How did you feel when your balloon dropped and you were helpless to do anything about it?

Study the Scripture

Read Psalm 10 aloud as a group antiphonal reading (alternate reading by two groups). Make sure all youth are using the same translation. Form two groups; one group reads aloud, in unison, the odd-numbered verses, and the other group reads aloud the even-numbered verses. Discuss using some or all of the questions from the Youth Study Book.

Read and Reflect

Read or review each section of the essay, using some or all of the following questions and activities.

Bart Simpson, Theologian?

- Does Bart's prayer offend you? Do you think it offends God? Why or why not?
- What other blessings from God can you think of that we can only experience if we do something to "help ourselves"?

The All-American Half Truth

- Are you surprised at how many people think the statement "God helps those who help themselves" is from the Bible? Why or why not?
- Do you agree that Americans "place a premium" on people helping themselves as stated in the Youth Study Book? Explain.

What This Half Truth Gets Right:
Personal Responsibility

- Have small groups of youth think of and pantomime other situations in which "simply waiting around for God's help isn't the best option."
- Obtain a copy of Dr. Seuss's *Oh, the Places You'll Go!* Read aloud the pages about "The Waiting Place."
- Arrange for youth to visit a children's class and read aloud (or act out) the Dr. Seuss book. Have youth talk with the children about when God expects us to help ourselves, and when we must wait for God to help us.
- How do you respond to one denomination's statement, "Life is a gift to be received with gratitude and a task to be pursued with courage"?

What This Half Truth Gets Wrong:
God, Helper of the Helpless

- Have youth use a concordance (in print or online) to find Bible verses and passages about God as helper of the helpless. Encourage them to choose a favorite verse on this subject and memorize it.

Will God Love Them Through Us?

- How does God's call to help the helpless challenge other values and priorities in American culture today?
- In what ways are you helping those who can't help themselves?

Suggested Activities

1. Acrostic Poetry

Publish youth's poems in your congregation's bulletin or newsletter, or on the church's or youth ministry's website (with each author's permission, of course).

2. Illustrate a Story of God's Help

Arrange for an exhibition of youth's art that other members of the congregation can attend.

3. Connect with a Helping Ministry

Invite a representative from a helping ministry or program, inside or outside of your congregation, to talk with youth about ways they can help.

4. Watch a Movie

The Soloist is rated PG-13; it contains moderate profanity and violence, and realistic depictions of the conditions faced by many people who experience homelessness. (See one reviewer's analysis of the content at http://www.kids-in-mind.com /s/soloist.htm.) The film is also a powerful story about society's responsibilities toward some of its most vulnerable members. Preview the film before deciding to watch it with your group. If you use it, show the entire film instead of isolated clips; youth will need the context of the whole story to discuss the questions in the Youth Study Book intelligently.

Daily Bible Readings

Encourage youth to follow these six-day schedules of readings in between sessions.

Session 3

GOD WON'T GIVE YOU MORE THAN YOU CAN HANDLE

Gather Around God's Word

This week's suggested hymn, "How Firm a Foundation," emphasizes God's trustworthy promises of comfort and strength during times of trouble. Its author is unknown, but it was first published in Baptist pastor John Rippon's *A Selection of Hymns from the Best Authors* (1787). The hymn was especially popular in both Union and Confederate states around the Civil War—certainly one of the nation's most "fiery trials." (To learn more, see C. Michael Hawn, "History of Hymns: 'How Firm a Foundation,'" http://www.umcdiscipleship.org/resources/history-of -hymns-how-firm-a-foundation.)

Getting Started

Serve as timekeeper when volunteers complete the various silly endurance challenges listed in the Youth Study Book. You might also invite them to think up and complete other challenges.

As an alternative icebreaker, have youth work in small teams of two to four people each to complete the first option under "Suggested Activities." For more details and in-depth teacher helps for such an activity, see the website listed in the Youth Study Book as well as TryEngineering's "Tall Tower Challenge" (http:// www.tryengineering.org/lessons/tower.pdf).

Study the Scripture

The following points may be helpful as you work through the study questions with youth:

- Consider recruiting volunteers to find and read aloud the passages from Exodus (see the first question) and Numbers (see the third question) before reading 1 Corinthians 10:1-13.

- Paul wants his readers to connect the church with the Israelites so they will regard God's judgment of the Israelites as a warning to them. Typology (where one thing is a "type"—a model, a pattern—of something that follows it later) helps Paul make this connection because, using it, he can find precedent in the Exodus story for the Christian practices of baptism and the Lord's Supper.
- Paul thinks he and his readers are living in the last days because God has raised Jesus from the dead. Some first-century Jews believed the general resurrection of the dead would precede the Messiah's coming and the arrival of God's kingdom. For Paul, Jesus' resurrection signaled the beginning of this resurrection of the dead.

Read and Reflect

Read or review each section of the essay, using some or all of the following questions and activities.

Big-Time Bible Blunders

- When have you heard people say, "God won't give you more than you can handle"? What kind of response did it get? How do you respond?

Tempting, Isn't It?

- Read 1 Corinthians 8 and paraphrase Paul's arguments for and against eating meat that had been sacrificed to idols. What issues in today's society present Christians with the same problems about deciding whether to participate?
- Is it always easy to recognize a "temptation to ungodly behavior"? Why or why not?

What This Half Truth Gets Right:
God Knows We Have Limits

- When have you been able to recognize and take a "way out" of temptation?
- Divide youth into small teams. Have each team think of and act out a situation in which someone is facing a temptation and is presented with a "way out." Stop each skit when the "way out" becomes clear, and have the whole group discuss the possible consequences of taking or not taking advantage of it.
- Unfortunately, the news usually has no shortage of stories about famous people who have been unable to resist temptation. Distribute

recent newspapers and magazines and have youth select such a story. Acknowledging that we may not know all the circumstances, how might things be different for this person if he or she had seen and taken a "way out" of temptation?

What This Half Truth Gets Wrong:
God Doesn't Pile On

- Do you think we can tell whether hard times are ever "given" to us by God—and, if so, how?
- What stories do you remember from the Gospels in which Jesus helped people who were living through tough times?

Suggested Activities

1. Build a Weight-Bearing Structure

See above, under "Getting Started." Be sure to take pictures or video of youths' structures for sharing via the church's or youth ministry's newsletters and websites!

2. Practice Lectio Divina

The method of *lectio divina* outlined here can be easily adapted to a group setting. Recruit three different volunteers to read the passage. After the first reading, simply have youth identify their chosen word, phrase, or image without further comment. After the subsequent two readings, you can allow time for further comment and questions from others.

3. Watch a Movie Clip

The scene described is chapter 49 of the theatrical edition DVD and disc 2, chapter 66 of the extended edition of *The Return of the King*.

4. Write an Encouraging Letter

In your next session, encourage youth to talk about what response, if any, they received after sending their letters.

Daily Bible Readings

Encourage youth to follow these six-day schedules of readings in between sessions.

Session 4

GOD SAID IT, I BELIEVE IT, THAT SETTLES IT

Gather Around God's Word

This week's suggested hymn, "O Word of God Incarnate," was written by William Walsham How, a nineteenth-century Anglican bishop who balanced a high view of the Bible's authority with an openness to the findings of modern science. (For more information, see C. Michael Hawn, "History of Hymns: 'O Word of God Incarnate,'" http://www.umcdiscipleship.org/resources/history-of -hymns-o-word-of-god-incarnate.) This hymn develops a rich view of the Word of God as both Scripture and the one to whom Scripture points, Jesus Christ, God's Word in the flesh. Youth may also know and enjoy singing "Thy Word" by Amy Grant and Michael W. Smith (© 1984 Meadowgreen Music).

Getting Started

Allow youth some time to read and react to the quotes printed in the Youth Study Book. If Internet access is available and time allows, have the group find additional interesting quotes about the Bible—positive, negative, and everything in between. Encourage youth to talk about which quotes interest, appeal to, or upset them, and why.

Study the Scripture

Recruit a volunteer to read aloud 2 Timothy 3. Discuss the passage using the questions from the Youth Study Book. Note that several of the questions involve comparing and contrasting the passage with other parts of Scripture. Youth may or may not arrive at fully satisfactory answers to questions about tensions in Scripture, but encourage them to be aware of such tensions and to continue to think and pray about them.

Read and Reflect

Read or review each section of the essay, using some or all of the following questions and activities.

No Cracks About "The Book"?

- How would you sum up the Bible's importance in ten words or fewer?
- What questions would other people have about the Bible that your summary leaves unanswered?
- What do you think people mean when they say, "God said it, I believe it, that settles it"?

"God Said It"?

- Have youth spend some time browsing their Bibles and noting as many different types and forms of literature within its pages as they can. What unites this variety of books, other than the fact that they're all now part of the Bible?
- In what sense, if at all, do you believe the Bible is God's Word?
- How is the sense in which Scripture is "inspired" the same as or different from the way we say, in casual conversation, that someone or something is "inspired"?
- What difference does it make that Christians believe God's Word became not a book but a person?

What This Half Truth Gets Right: "I Believe It"

- Read statements of faith from your denomination or tradition about the nature and importance of Scripture. What do youth agree with in these statements? What do they have questions about?
- Summarize, in your own words, the difference between *general revelation* and *special revelation*. How important, if at all, is this difference in your understanding of Christian faith?
- Do you think it's possible to treat the Bible too seriously? Why or why not?

What This Half Truth Gets Wrong: "That Settles It"

- What are some differences among the three beliefs about the Bible—inerrant, infallible, or inspired—that are held by most Christians? Which of these positions, if any, do you hold and why?

- How have you heard the Bible used to "settle" a disagreement instead of used to keep a conversation going? What happened?
- If you think your group is mature enough for the assignment, identify a controversial topic from church or society—perhaps one mentioned in the essay, perhaps another. What positions have youth heard Christians take on this issue? What Scriptures can youth identify that support or challenge these positions?

Suggested Activities

1. Make a Bible Bookmark

Consider having youth distribute their bookmarks to members of the congregation who are homebound or hospitalized.

2. Blow Up a "Bible Balloon"

In addition to writing on the outside of the uninflated balloon, youth could also write their chosen Bible verses on small slips of paper and insert the verses into the balloons before blowing up the balloons. Ask your worship leadership if the balloons could be used to decorate the congregation's worship space in an upcoming service.

3. Watch a Movie Clip

Inherit the Wind (1960) is available on DVD and from legal online streaming video sources. Encourage youth to answer at least the last question in the Youth Study Book, identifying modern situations in which people disagree about how to read the Bible.

4. Donate a Bible

Consider planning a group fundraiser in order to donate several Bibles to the ministry of your choosing.

Daily Bible Readings

Encourage youth to follow these six-day schedules of readings in between sessions.

Session 5

LOVE THE SINNER, HATE THE SIN

Gather Around God's Word

This week's suggested hymn, "Amazing Grace," is a familiar one that youth may even know without needing printed lyrics or music (at least for the first verse). They may also be familiar with the history of the hymn: how Captain John Newton, commander of a slave ship, had a conversion experience during a storm and eventually became a pastor who helped William Wilberforce end the British slave trade.[1] The first verse's use of the word *wretch* connects well with this session's theme: we ought not be self-righteous "saints" who generously "love the sinner," but wretches who—saved only by God's grace—love our neighbors. Youth may enjoy the arrangement, "Amazing Grace (My Chains are Gone)" by Chris Tomlin, from his 2006 album, *See the Morning*.

Getting Started

Allow youth time to complete the word search printed in the Youth Study Book.

As an alternative or additional icebreaker, form small teams of youth, distribute magazines and newspapers, and give the teams exactly seven minutes to find stories and pictures illustrating as many of the "seven deadly sins" as possible. Give each team one point per sin illustrated; give bonus points if a story or picture illustrates more than one sin. At the end of the activity, collect all the stories and pictures and throw them into a recycling bin, reminding youth that God calls Christians to flee from sin!

---

1. See "John Newton, Reformed Slave Trader," August 8, 2008, http://www.christianitytoday.com/ch /131christians/pastorsandpreachers/newton.html?start=1.

Study the Scripture

Recruit a volunteer to read aloud Jesus' words in Matthew 7:1-5, and recruit two others to pantomime the words as they are read. The broader and more comical the pantomime, the better!

Read and Reflect

Read or review each section of the essay, using some or all of the following questions and activities.

Everyone Else a Sinner?

- When have you heard people say, "Love the sinner, hate the sin"?
- What about this statement may make it a half truth? What about it may be hurtful to the speaker or the listener?

Jesus' Serious Joke

- Do you tend to think of Jesus as having a sense of humor? Why or why not?
- Give youth time to complete the suggestion of illustrating Matthew 7:1-5 (especially if your group did not use the pantomime option under "Study the Scripture").
- Show youth the visual lesson: point your finger accusingly at someone, then show that your pointing hand now has three fingers pointing back at yourself. Suggest that this illustrates the situation we find ourselves in when we try to "love the sinner, hate the sin"—we become hypocrites, accusing ourselves more than the people we are judging.

What This Half Truth Gets Right:
Sin Is Serious

- Have youth use a concordance, a computer, or an online Bible search to find other verses commanding God's people to flee from sin. Encourage youth to memorize at least one of the verses they find.
- Explain, in your own words, the difference Paul saw between sins and the power of sin.

What This Half Truth Gets Wrong:
Neighbors, Not "Sinners"

- What is the difference between "loving the sinner" and "loving the neighbor"?

- How have you seen "God's Spirit...at work to make [our neighbors and us] holy, as God is holy"?

Truth and Love

- What is the most helpful insight you have gained from our study of *Half Truths*?
- What is one question you still have about a half truth from this study? What is your follow-up plan for answering the question?

Suggested Activities

1. Study Scriptures About Sin

Have youth work in pairs or small groups to complete this activity.

2. Write a Prayer of Confession

Consult with pastoral leadership and worship planners about using written and visual prayers of confession in an upcoming worship service, with each youth's permission.

3. Make and Share Friendship Bread

If you want to have friendship bread ready to eat with your students, you will need to allow ten days' preparation time; consult recipes online for details. This might make an especially good intergenerational activity: children can help youth mix the ingredients and adults can help youth bake the bread.

4. Reflect on the Face of Love

As the Youth Study Book notes, *Dead Man Walking* is rated R. As leader, you must decide whether your group should watch the scene described. It begins at about 1:35:03 (Matt: "That boy...") and ends at about 1:42:20 (when the guard shouts, "Dead man walking!"). Use your best judgment when deciding whether to show the scene. It contains no foul language from the point indicated (some precedes that point), but does contain one reference to rape (Sister Helen: "Did you rape her?"), and may be a situation too upsetting for some youth, particularly younger youth. On the other hand, the scene remains one of the most powerful and moving portrayals of Christian ministry and love found in film.

Daily Bible Readings

Encourage youth to follow these six-day schedules of readings in between sessions.

YOUTH STUDY BOOK

INTRODUCTION

Everybody knows that in the classic movie *Casablanca*, Humphrey Bogart says, "Play it again, Sam."

Except he doesn't. (He really says, "Play it, Sam.")

Everybody knows that one of Captain Kirk's most famous lines in the *Star Trek* series is "Beam me up, Scotty."

Except he never says it. (He comes close once, in the movie *Star Trek IV*—"Scotty, beam me up"—but that was in 1986, after "Beam me up, Scotty" had a been a pop culture mainstay for twenty years.)

Everybody knows that Sherlock Holmes likes to say, "Elementary, my dear Watson."

Except the great detective never says that, not once in any of Sir Arthur Conan Doyle's fifty-six short stories and four novels about him. (Holmes says one or the other half of the line a number of times, but never together.)

In the same way, there are a lot of things that "everybody knows" the Bible says.

Except sometimes it doesn't.

The Bible never says, "Everything happens for a reason." Or "God helps those who help themselves." Or "God won't give you more than you can handle." The Bible also never claims to be the direct and unmediated Word of God. And it never says that Jesus told us, "Love the sinner, hate the sin."

All these ideas are half truths that creep into many Christians' faith. The problem is not so much that the statements are wrong as that they're just not

1

quite right enough. Taken at face value, and taken to extremes, they can lead to mistaken beliefs about God, Jesus, and our fellow human beings. Wrong beliefs can lead to wrong practice.

Wrong beliefs can also prove painful. Many times, we tell people these things with nothing but the best of intentions. We fully intend to love our neighbor by offering helpful and comforting words. But because these words aren't fully true, they can end up causing a lot of damage. The words might cause other people, if they have faith, to stumble in their beliefs. If the other people don't have faith, these half truths might prove a roadblock in their ever coming to faith. And, in either case, these statements might damage relationships. If you say something hurtful to someone, even when you didn't mean to, that person may be less likely to stay connected to you going forward, for fear she or he will be hurt again.

In this study—based on Adam Hamilton's book *Half Truths*—you will examine some half truths...things that "everybody knows" the Bible says, except it doesn't. You'll discover what each half truth gets right and what it gets wrong. By the time we're done, maybe you'll have a better handle on what Scripture really leads us to believe and do, and how to live as a truthful disciples of the one who promised his Spirit would lead us into all truth, Jesus Christ.

1.

EVERYTHING HAPPENS
FOR A REASON

*[Then Moses said to the Israelites,] "I call heaven and earth to
witness against you today that I have set before you life and death,
blessings and curses. Choose life so that you and your descendants
may live, loving the LORD your God, obeying him, and holding fast
to him; for that means life to you and length of days."*
—Deuteronomy 30:19-20a NRSV

Gather Around God's Word

Lead me in your truth—teach it to me—because you are the God who saves me.
I put my hope in you all day long.

(Psalm 25:5)

3

Open the Bible and light a candle.

God of truth, we admit your ways often seem hidden from us, and we confess we often claim more knowledge of your will than we actually possess. May your Spirit guide us to humbly seek signs of your work. Help us place less trust in our own wisdom and more trust in your Son, Jesus Christ, who became wisdom from you for us, to make us righteous and holy and to save us. Amen.

Sing or read "Be Still, My Soul" (words by Katharina von Schlegel)

Jesus said, "You are truly my disciples if you remain faithful to my teaching. Then you will know the truth, and the truth will set you free." (John 8:31-32)

Jesus said, "I am the way, the truth, and the life. No one comes to the Father except through me." (John 14:6)

Getting Started

Spend some time browsing recent issues of your local newspaper or a magazine focused on current events and/or some local, national, and world news websites. Clip or copy two or three headlines that grab your attention. Spread them before you and look at them as you think about these questions:

- Which, if any, of these headlines make sense to you? Which ones agree with your understanding of how the world works, or ought to work?
- Which, if any, of these headlines leave you shaking your head and asking why?
- In which, if any, of these headlines do you think you see glimpses of God at work? Why?
- What do you imagine Jesus would say if he were reading these headlines with you?

Study the Scripture

Read Deuteronomy 30:11-21. Moses is addressing the Israelites at the end of their forty years of wandering in the wilderness, just before they enter the land God has promised them as their new home.

- In your own words, what is Moses' main message to the Israelites? What does he want them to do?

- What reasons does Moses give for the Israelites to do what he is telling them? (See especially verses 11-14, 16.)
- What consequences will the Israelites face if they fail to do what Moses tells them? (See especially verses 17-18.)
- In your experience, how easy or difficult is it to do what Moses is telling the Israelites to do? Can you talk about a time when you either did or did not make the choice Moses wants them to make? What happened?
- Do you think Moses' message accurately explains why we experience "blessing and curse" (verse 19)? Why or why not?
- How much freedom do you think God gives us to choose what we do and what happens to us? Explain your answer.

Read and Reflect

Do We Choose Our Own Adventures?

In middle school, my favorite books were the *Choose Your Own Adventure* series. In these books, "you" are the hero—sometimes an ordinary kid in such extraordinary circumstances as a haunted house or a lost civilization; sometimes someone more exotic like an astronaut, secret agent, or circus performer. "You" start reading on page 1, but what pages you turn to next depends on how you respond to various decision points in the text.

Some choices are pretty routine stuff: "If you go west, turn to page 5. If you head east, turn to page 13." But other choices seem more consequential. Will you trust the mysterious wizard to lead you out of the cave? Turn to page 29. Will you tell the unidentified alien ship that you welcome it in peace? Turn to page 42.

I never felt really satisfied unless I got to make at least a dozen choices before hitting those dreaded words in bold face at the bottom of the page: The End (usually preceded by "your" sudden, terrible demise).

Choose Your Own Adventure books can be a lot of fun, but the series title is a little misleading. Sure, you make decisions that affect how you read the plot—but the book's author has determined in advance all the choices and their consequences. Everything that happens in these books, including every single forced choice the reader makes, is put there for a reason—the writer's reason, not yours.

Thankfully, in real life we really get to "choose our own adventures," right? While none of us have completely blank pages handed to us at birth—we can't control where or to whom we're born, for example, or whether we're born in good health—we're more or less free to make our own choices and write our life stories for ourselves. Aren't we?

Not if you believe this half truth Christians often say they believe: "Everything happens for a reason."

What This Half Truth Gets Right: God Cares and God Rules

People often tell this half truth to themselves and others when everything is going badly—*really* badly. A loved one dies. A storm does terrible damage. A job is lost. "It's sad and terrible," they'll say, "but, even if we can't understand it now, we have to believe it happened for a reason."

This half truth is what theologians call a *theodicy* (*thee-ODD-ih-see*), a defense of God's goodness and power in the face of what could be evidence to the contrary.

Try and think about the following three statements, all of which Christians claim are true, all at once:

1. God is all-loving.
2. God is all-powerful.
3. Suffering exists.

If all these statements are true, how can an all-loving, all-powerful God let suffering happen?

- Maybe God *is* all-loving but not powerful enough to stop our suffering. But is a god who is powerless against suffering the God we read about in the Exodus, or in stories of Jesus healing sick people?
- Maybe God *is* all-powerful but doesn't really love us, meaning God is content to let us suffer. But Scripture shows us a God whose love leads to the relief and ultimate end of suffering. (For example, see the description of God's promised future in Revelation 21:4.)
- Maybe suffering is an illusion. That conclusion seems to fly in the face of millennia of human experience, but at least it keeps God's hands clean. Some world religions do teach that suffering isn't real, but classic Christianity never has taught that—how could it, when Jesus suffered and died?

No single theodicy satisfactorily juggles all three of those statements at once. And, as theodicies go, "Everything happens for a reason" is better than some.

It avoids two big theological mistakes: atheism, which claims there is no god, and deism, which affirms God's existence but claims that God took a "hands-off" approach to the world once God finished creating it.

The idea that "everything happens for a reason" agrees with biblical teaching that God cares about and stays involved with the world. It's really a statement about God's providence. Here's something you can impress your teachers with: The word *providence* comes from the Latin prefix *pro*, "before," and the verb *video*, "to see." God sees what is best for us, and provides accordingly.

If you had been a young Protestant Christian in sixteenth-century Germany, you might have had to memorize and recite this definition of God's providence:

> The almighty and ever present power of God by which God upholds, as with his hand, heaven and earth and all creatures, and so rules them that leaf and blade, rain and drought, fruitful and lean years, food and drink, health and sickness, prosperity and poverty—all things, in fact, come to us not by chance but by his fatherly hand. [1]

There's no question the Bible teaches about God's providence. The psalm-singer praises God for feeding people and wild animals alike (Psalm 104). Jesus said if God can be trusted to give birds food and wildflowers beauty, then God can also be trusted to give us what we need (Matthew 6:25-32). But do "all things" come to us *directly* from God's hand? Is random chance really never at work? Does God actually choose who will get good weather and who will get bad, who will grow rich and who will stay poor? Does God ever cause bad things to happen?

What This Half Truth Gets Wrong: It Can Paralyze Us and Hurt Others

If we press this view of providence too far, we end up with a god who looks less like a loving parent and more like a *Choose Your Own Adventure* writer. If "everything happens for a reason" in a divinely micromanaged way, then we *aren't* really free, and our choices *don't* really matter, because God has already plotted our lives down to the last page.

A belief that God has plotted our lives and everything else for a reason could suck a lot of wind out of our sails.

- Why study for that algebra test? God has already decided if you'll get an *A* or an *F*.

- Why work up the nerve to ask that good-looking girl or guy to prom? If God has picked out a soul mate for you, she or he will show up when God is good and ready.
- Why should fast-food employees demand a higher minimum wage? God has already determined their earning potential and place in life.
- Why should we race for cures, wear rubber bracelets, and issue ice bucket challenges to raise money for disease research? Whether you make it through life with a clean bill of health is up to the divine doctor, isn't it?

If we're not careful, the idea that "everything happens for a reason" can leave us paralyzed and passive before a god who's holding all the cards, who moves us around like characters in a book for purposes unknown and unknowable.

Besides paralyzing us, the saying can hurt others. Does the tragic death of a parent or sibling or friend really "happen for a reason"? In using this saying to help friends who are suffering, we can inadvertently cause them pain, because these words seem to imply that God caused the tragedy, that God manipulates us like chess pieces for unknown purposes. Because of this implication, using the saying with friends might actually damage their faith in a time when they need it most.

Beyond theodicy, beyond logic, beyond definitions, Christ calls us to love. When we use the half truth "Everything happens for a reason," there's a possibility that instead we will hurt others.

Really Choosing God

Deuteronomy 30 gives us another way of thinking about God's providence. The Israelites, who used to be slaves in Egypt, are about to enter the Promised Land. Moses tells them they have a serious decision to make: they can choose to obey God and build their community according to God's will *or* they can choose to go it alone, ignoring God's guidance, following make-believe gods in hopes that those gods will bring blessing. One choice leads to life; the other, to death.

Moses urges the Israelites to choose life by choosing God. God has seen what is best for God's people and has provided; God has freed them and brought them to a new home. But God hasn't robbed them of their ability—their *responsibility*—to make choices that matter.

God's commandments aren't arbitrary rules designed to make life less fun. They show us how we are most likely to experience God's goodness: by worshiping God, by telling the truth and keeping our promises, by respecting and loving our neighbors. When we make these kinds of choices, choices that line up with God's priorities and values, we're more likely to choose adventures in which we "live and thrive" (Deuteronomy 30:16), as God wants us to.

Of course, choosing these adventures isn't as simple as turning to one page instead of another. Godly choices don't always lead immediately to good outcomes; think of the martyrs throughout Christian history—and even today, in some parts of the world—who lose their homes, their jobs, even their lives because they remain faithful to God. And not all people who suffer bring it on themselves. Sometimes wrong choices affect other people more than they do the person who made them; sometimes bad things do happen by chance.

God doesn't make everything happen for a reason—but God can bring meaning out of anything that happens. "We know," wrote the apostle Paul, "that God works all things together for good for the ones who love God, for those who are called according to his purpose" (Romans 8:28). Nothing that happens, and no choice we make, can ultimately derail the great adventure God has chosen for us and for all creation, because "nothing can separate us from God's love in Christ Jesus our Lord" (Romans 8:38).

Suggested Activities

1. It's a Good Thing/Bad Thing

Play this improvisational performance game with a partner: One of you starts the game by announcing some crazy, make-believe event (for example, "My neighbor's house was swallowed by a dinosaur last night"). Your partner gives a reason why the event was a good thing ("That's good; now the dinosaur won't go hungry"). You respond with a reason why it was a bad thing ("But now my neighbor has no place to live"). Your partner responds with another positive ("Your neighbor can move wherever she wants to"); you respond with another negative ("But the dinosaur will follow her wherever she goes")—and so on, and so on…the more outrageous, the better.

- How is this game like and unlike people trying to determine why and whether "everything happens for a reason"?

2. Watch a Movie

Signs (Touchstone Pictures, 2002; directed by M. Night Shyamalan) is about a former pastor, Graham (played by Mel Gibson), who discovers mysterious crop circles on his farm. Soon, strange lights start appearing in night skies around the world. Graham struggles not only to protect himself and his family from extraterrestrial invaders but also to make sense out of confusing, unresolved events from his past and present.

In one scene, Graham tells his brother: "See, what you have to ask yourself is, what kind of person are you? Are you the kind who sees signs, sees miracles? Or do you believe that people just get lucky?"

- Which kind of person do you tend to be? Why?
- What answers, if any, does this movie give to the question, "Does everything happen for a reason?" Do you agree with its answers? Why or why not?

3. Plot a Personal Timeline

On a separate piece of paper, plot some major events of your life on a timeline. Illustrate it if you wish, with sketches or photos. Now modify your timeline in these ways:

- Draw a square around events you had no control over.
- Draw a diamond around events that were shaped, to some extent, by your choices; above or below those events, jot down notes about the choice you made, why you made it, and what you imagine might have happened had you made different choices.
- Draw a cross at those points, if any, when you were confident you felt God's guidance.
- Draw a question mark at those points, if any, when you were less sure of God's presence.

If you feel comfortable doing so, talk about your timeline with a Christian friend you trust.

4. Make a Mobile

Mount headlines and pictures clipped from newspapers and magazines to circles and squares cut from construction paper. Cut various lengths of string or yarn; tape one end of each length to the back of the construction paper and tie the loose ends to a wire coat hanger. Experiment with adding and removing paper clips to the construction paper in order to make the mobile as balanced as possible.

- How do you think your mobile might be an image of how God is at work in the events of our world and our lives?

Daily Bible Readings

Day 1: Genesis 3:1-13

Some people argue that God is ultimately responsible for human sin. Why did God put a forbidden tree in Eden in the first place? Didn't God *know* Adam and Eve would eat its fruit? Do you think God is somehow to blame for what happened? What does this story tell you about human beings' freedom and responsibility to make choices?

Day 2: Job 2:1-10

Job accepted all his suffering as "from God" (verse 10)—patiently in these verses, but not so much in most of the book! Can we thank God for the good in our lives without also blaming God for the bad? Have you ever demanded God tell you why bad things happen, as Job demands in the rest of the book? What happened?

Day 3: Ecclesiastes 9:1-12

The author of Ecclesiastes didn't believe that "everything happens for a reason" but did write a lot about how random chance and death affect everyone, good or bad. What do you think of his advice for living? Can you believe that some things "just happen" and at the same time believe that Jesus' resurrection changes our attitude toward death?

Day 4: Luke 13:1-5

The people around Jesus want to find a deeper meaning in Pontius Pilate's murder of people as they worshiped at the Temple. Jesus rejects their conclusion about this event, as well as another one—a tower's sudden collapse—and says the people should draw a different lesson. What choice does Jesus say tragedies and disasters like these should motivate people to make?

Day 5: John 9:1-7

People in Jesus' day often assumed a direct link between personal suffering and sin. How does Jesus challenge this commonly made connection in the case of the man born blind? Do you think Jesus' words in verse 3 mean that God *caused* the man's blindness or *used* it? Why? When have you seen personal hardships (your own or someone else's) bring glory to God?

Day 6: Romans 8:26-39

How can each of the truths that the Apostle Paul discusses in these verses encourage us as we think about the mystery of why things happen: The Holy Spirit's prayers for us? God's ability to make all things work for good? God's knowing, calling, and saving us? The strength of God's love for us in Jesus Christ?

2.

GOD HELPS THOSE
WHO HELP THEMSELVES

The helpless commit themselves to you; you have been the helper of the orphan.... O LORD, you will hear the desire of the meek; you will strengthen their heart, you will incline your ear to do justice for the orphan and the oppressed.

—Psalm 10:14b, 17-18a NRSV

Gather Around God's Word

Make your ways known to me, LORD; teach me your paths.

Lead me in your truth—teach it to me—because you are the God who saves me.

(Psalm 25:4-5)

Open the Bible and light a candle.

God of truth, you command us to practice the pure and spotless religion of helping other people in their distress. By your Spirit, strengthen us to hear your call to serve and to respond, believing that when we help those who are helpless, we are helping your Son, Jesus Christ, who helped while we were still sinners, giving his life that we might live. Amen.

Sing or read "Grace Alone" (Scott Wesley Brown and Jeff Nelson, © 1998 Maranatha! Music)

Jesus said… "You are truly my disciples if you remain faithful to my teaching. Then you will know the truth, and the truth will set you free." (John 8:31-32)

Jesus answered, "I am the way, the truth, and the life. No one comes to the Father except through me." (John 14:6)

Getting Started

- Sit in a straight-backed chair with your feet flat on the floor and your arms folded across your chest so that your hands are on your shoulders. What happens when you try to stand up without leaning forward?
- Place your hand on a table, fingers splayed (as though you were going to trace your hand). Fold your middle finger backward so that it is touching your palm. Raise and lower your thumb. Raise and lower your index (pointer) finger. Raise and lower your pinky. What happens when you try to raise and lower your ring finger?

These situations should leave you helpless—unable to do what is asked of you—but only temporarily and in a very specific way.

When is a time when you have *really* felt helpless? What did you do about it? What happened?

Study the Scripture

Read Psalm 10.

- What is the psalm-singer's complaint?
- What evidence does the psalm-singer cite that supports this complaint?

- How does the psalm-singer want God to respond?
- Describe the shift in the psalm-singer's attitude from the beginning of the psalm to its end. Why do you think this shift happens?
- Talk about a time when you felt, as the psalm-singer does, that God was standing far off. How did you handle that experience?
- How comfortable are you expressing feelings of helplessness to God in prayer?
- What Bible stories can you think of that support the psalm-singer's words to God, "You do see troublemaking and grief, and you do something about it!" (verse 14)?
- How have you personally experienced God helping you or someone you know?
- What people in your community need help so that they "will never again be terrified" (verse 18)?
- Bible scholars say Psalms 9 and 10 are probably meant to be a single psalm. How does Psalm 9 apply Psalm 10's lessons about how God helps, from individuals to the lives of whole nations? How do you think nations today need to remember and respond to the truth that real help comes from God?

Read and Reflect

Bart Simpson, Theologian?

Hard as it may be to believe now, when *The Simpsons* debuted in 1989 it was controversial. Well-meaning grownups wrung their hands about how it would corrupt America's youth. I remember my pastor denouncing from the pulpit one episode that he believed mocked common decency in general and Christian faith in particular.

In the episode, the Simpsons are hosting Homer's boss for dinner. Homer desperately wants his family to make a good impression. He asks Bart—the rebellious kid best known at the time for telling people to "eat my shorts"—to say the mealtime grace. Bart folds his hands and bows his head, then prays, "Dear God, we paid for all this stuff ourselves, so thanks for nothing."

My pastor was scandalized, but I thought the scene was funny. Because, let's face it—Bart has a point. God didn't do the grocery shopping. Human beings made the meal happen. Maybe you personally didn't do anything to get your food today, but plenty of other people did. Farmers grew the grains, harvested the produce, raised the animals. Truckers moved goods to processing plants and grocery stores. Someone purchased and prepped what's on your plate. So why give God a shout-out?

We thank God because, in the psalm-singer's words, God "make[s] grass grow for cattle…[and] plants for human farming in order to get food from the ground" (Psalm 104:14-15). God gave us life and a world capable of sustaining it. When Jesus taught his disciples to pray for their daily bread, he wasn't teaching them that God makes food show up by magic. He was teaching that, whenever we help ourselves to food, we're only able to do so because God helped us first.

All blessings flow from God, but frequently they flow through a divine-human partnership. That's the truth Bart Simpson's prayer can teach us.

The All-American Half Truth

The truth Bart Simpson can teach us, however, has been cut in half. It's become a saying so familiar that over 75 percent of American teens think it's a Bible verse: "God helps those who help themselves."[2]

This half truth has been part of the United States' religious thinking since our nation's beginning. As a result, we tend to place a premium on people helping themselves. Although the sentiment predates Christianity, we have Benjamin Franklin to thank for its widely known form. He put it in *Poor Richard's Almanac*,[3] his collection of pithy proverbs that offered eighteenth-century readers what we might today call "life hacks," hints for happiness and success.

As practical advice goes, this half truth isn't all bad. Even before Franklin, early Americans had discovered its value. One example: The winter of 1609–1610 was bitter for English colonists in Jamestown, Virginia. Food was scarce during "the Starving Time." Recent archaeological excavations revealed that settlers even resorted to eating dogs, cats, horses—and at least one dead fourteen-year-old girl.[4] (Did your American history teacher ever tell you *that*?) To give the colony a shot at survival, its leader, Captain John Smith, decreed, "[Y]ou must obey this now for a Law, that he that will not work shall not eat."[5] Smith's law echoed a rule the Apostle Paul laid down for an early Christian congregation: "If anyone doesn't want to work, they shouldn't eat" (2 Thessalonians 3:10). The experience could be considered a case study in the practical benefit of believing that "God helps those who help themselves."

What This Half Truth Gets Right: Personal Responsibility

You're probably not facing any circumstances as dire as those faced by the colonists in Jamestown. But you may be in situations where simply waiting around for God's help isn't the best option.

- God *could* miraculously grant you better grades on your report card—but regular attendance, completed homework, and hard studying are all better bets.
- God *could* make a college acceptance letter or a job offer fall from heaven—but, honestly, you won't go to the school of your choice or get the work you want without submitting applications.
- God *could* give you perfect health and a fit physique while you sleep—but making healthy food choices and exercising regularly are surefire ways to get into shape.

People who wait around for God to act without acting themselves are like the folk in Dr. Seuss's *Oh, the Places You'll Go!* who are stuck in "The Waiting Place," where *nothing* happens because no one is *making* anything happen. Everyone is depending upon someone or something else to take the initiative ... or even just for something to occur at random ... or for some vague undefined something that may never come at all. They're waiting "perhaps, for their Uncle Jake / or a pot to boil, or a Better Break." And as they wait, they forget that—to paraphrase Seuss—God gave us brains in our heads and feet in our shoes, to steer ourselves any direction we choose.[6]

I like what one denomination's statement of faith says about human existence: "Life is a gift to be received with gratitude and a task to be pursued with courage."[7] If you have big dreams and grand plans, by all means pray about them—but don't expect God to hand you results wrapped with a shiny bow in response. You are responsible for *doing* something about what you want your life to be. Get out there and help yourself!

What This Half Truth Gets Wrong: God, Helper of the Helpless

Unfortunately, this half truth leads us in the wrong direction when we assume that God *only* helps people who help themselves. The Bible consistently witnesses to a different truth: God *especially* helps people who *cannot* help themselves.

Psalm 10 is one of many biblical texts celebrating God's help for the helpless. We don't know who first sings this psalm, but he or she feels under attack from more powerful foes. Enemies are laying traps and plotting not only against the psalm-singer but also against society's most vulnerable members: people in poverty, children without parents, all those on the social sidelines whose lack of money and influence means their protests against corruption and injustice go unheard. These "helpless victims are crushed," the psalm-singer laments; "they collapse, falling prey to the strength of the wicked" (Psalm 10:10).

But there is hope! The psalm-singer believes God will make things right: "You do see troublemaking and grief, and you do something about it!" (verse 14). God will "listen closely" to the victims of wickedness, and will "establish justice for the orphan and the oppressed" (verse 18).

Plenty of people who are poor show up in Scripture, but the Bible spends little time wondering how they became poor or what they should do about it. "Thou shalt get a job" isn't one of the Ten Commandments, and "Blessed are they who pull themselves up by their own bootstraps" isn't one of Jesus' Beatitudes. What the Bible *does* talk about is how God helps people who are poor, sick, orphaned, weak, or in any way left to fend for themselves on the margins.

God "gives justice to people who are oppressed…gives bread to people who are starving…frees prisoners…makes the blind see…straightens up those who are bent low…protects immigrants…helps orphans and widows…[and] makes the way of the wicked twist and turn!" (Psalm 146:7-9).

What's more, the Bible talks a lot about how God wants to send this help to the helpless *through us*.

Will God Love Them Through Us?

Let me tell you about another pastor from my youth, who worried about something a lot more substantial.

Our congregation's big, historic building was downtown in a major city. Many members lived in nicer parts of town, or even in the suburbs, and drove downtown for worship and other activities. Not many, my family included, lived near the church's immediate neighbors who dealt with poverty, crime, homelessness, drugs, and other familiar urban challenges.

An opportunity came for the church to buy a vacant building next door and transform it into a community services center. Some on the church board were skeptical. There were so many other things, things the church needed or wanted, that the money could be spent on. And serving free meals every now and then to people in poverty was fine, but getting involved with them in-depth, in an on-

18

going way—providing food and clothing and shelter but also literacy classes, job training, medical care—well, was the church really called to make all that happen?

I didn't see it for myself, but I'm told my pastor listened quietly to all the objections raised by the board members around the table, then leaned forward, peered at them intently over the top of his glasses, and said, "God is going to love this city. The only question is, Will God love this city through us?"

The plan passed, and even today that church is a leader in providing emergency and ongoing assistance to people who cannot help themselves.

Whenever we help people who cannot help themselves, we reflect and spread the love of God: "God shows his love for us, because while we were still sinners Christ died for us" (Romans 5:8). God is gracious, which is another way of saying God helps the helpless, including you and me. God "brought us to life with Christ while we were dead as a result" of our sins—"You are saved by God's grace!" (Ephesians 2:5). God saves us by grace, not only for an eternity in God's presence but also for a life, here and now, of helping those who cannot help themselves.

Suggested Activities

1. Acrostic Poetry

Bible scholars point out that in the original Hebrew, Psalms 9 and 10 were probably a single psalm. The combined psalm is a loose acrostic poem: every second poetic line (except in 10:3-6) starts with a letter of the Hebrew alphabet, moving through the alphabet from start to finish (but some letters are missing). Write your own acrostic poem about how you have experienced God's help, and ways you have helped or plan to help others in response. Use the letters of your name, or a meaningful word or phrase, as the basis for your poem; or follow the psalm-singer's lead and use all or a portion of the alphabet.

2. Illustrate a Story of God's Help

Scripture has no shortage of stories about God helping people who cannot help themselves. Select one of these stories to illustrate—write and draw a comic book, make a diorama, paint a watercolor. Whatever medium you choose, clearly show how God's help made a difference. Some stories to consider:

- God makes a promise to Hagar (Genesis 16)
- The Israelites cross the Red Sea (Exodus 14)
- God sends manna in the wilderness (Exodus 16)

- Daniel in the lions' den (Daniel 6)
- Jesus stills a stormy sea (Mark 4:35-41)
- Jesus helps the woman accused of adultery (John 8:1-11)

3. Connect with a Helping Ministry

Get involved, if you aren't already, with some ongoing ministry or program that offers help to people who need it. Your youth ministry and congregation may already support such programs; you could also look outside your congregation to community assistance programs, local charities, and so on. Commit to helping for more than one or a few occasions; pick a program you can stick with for some time. Keep a journal or blog/vlog about your experiences. What new things did you learn about how to help people?

4. Watch a Movie

The Soloist (2009, rated PG-13) is based on the true story of journalist Steve Lopez (played by Robert Downey Jr.) who meets a former Juilliard music student, Nathaniel Ayers (Jamie Foxx), who has become homeless; Nathaniel lives under a Los Angeles freeway, playing the violin. Steve decides he will try to help Nathaniel improve his life.

- How does Steve try to help Nathaniel? What do you think about Steve's motivations?
- Do you think Steve ends up helping Nathaniel? Why?
- How does Steve say Nathaniel ends up helping him?
- In what ways does this film define and illustrate the meaning of grace?
- What lessons can Christians learn from *The Soloist* about what helping people means and looks like in practice?
- Do you think *The Soloist* affirms or challenges the idea that "God helps those who help themselves"—or does it do some of each? Explain.

Daily Bible Readings

Day 1: Psalm 121

Bible scholars think ancient pilgrims on their way to worship at the Temple in Jerusalem would sing this psalm as they prepared for the long journey up Mount

Zion. How have you experienced God helping you during the "pilgrimage" that is your life? In what ways has God protected you?

Day 2: Exodus 14:10-18

The story of the Exodus, the fundamental story that shaped ancient Israel's faith, is all about God helping people who could not help themselves. How do experiences of God's help involve both staying still (verse 14) and being on the move (verse 15)? How does helping the helpless bring glory to God?

Day 3: Leviticus 19:1, 9-10

For ancient Israel, being "holy" didn't mean being "holier than thou." Holiness meant doing things that marked Israelites as radically different from others, set apart for a special purpose. How do these laws about harvesting crops mark ancient Israel as holy? What are some modern practices that you think are equivalent to leaving the harvest's leftovers to help those who are hungry?

Day 4: John 15:1-5

Why does Jesus use the metaphor of a vine and its branches to describe his relationship to his disciples? What "fruit" have you been able to produce because of your connection to Christ? Have you ever experienced for yourself the truth of his words, "Without me, you can't do anything" (verse 5)? What happened?

Day 5: James 1:22-27

For the apostle James, true religion is a matter of correct action, not simply correct belief (see 2:19!). Widows and orphans were some of first-century society's most vulnerable members; they are still often among the most vulnerable today. What other people in your community are in special need of help? How will you and your youth ministry or congregation help them?

Day 6: Romans 5:6-11

God did not wait until we could help ourselves to help us in Jesus Christ! What are the results of God's acts for us in Jesus, according to the Apostle Paul? This week, how will you reflect your "restored relationship" with God (verse 11) in acts of helping others?

3.

GOD WON'T GIVE YOU
MORE THAN YOU CAN HANDLE

*No temptation has seized you that isn't common for people. But
God is faithful. He won't allow you to be tempted beyond your
abilities. Instead, with the temptation, God will also supply a way
out so that you will be able to endure it.*

—1 Corinthians 10:13

Gather Around God's Word

Make your ways known to me, LORD; teach me your paths.

Lead me in your truth—teach it to me—because you are the God who saves me.

(Psalm 25:4-5)

Open the Bible and light a candle.

God of truth, you don't willingly afflict anyone, and you shower your compassion over all that you have made. When we face any kind of temptation or trouble, may your Spirit move us to look to and trust in you, for you have shared and overcome human suffering in your crucified and risen Son, Jesus Christ. Amen.

Sing or read "How Firm a Foundation" (from Rippon's Selection of Hymns, 1787)

Jesus said … "You are truly my disciples if you remain faithful to my teaching. Then you will know the truth, and the truth will set you free." (John 8:31-32)

Jesus [said], "I am the way, the truth, and the life. No one comes to the Father except through me." (John 14:6)

Getting Started

How long can you…

- Run in place?
- Stand in one place?
- Keep a blown-up balloon in the air by batting it around?
- Do a crab walk?
- Spin in a circle without falling down (or making yourself sick!)?

Write down your times, compare them with someone else's—and get ready to think about some more serious forms of endurance.

Study the Scripture

Read 1 Corinthians 10:1-13.

- According to Paul, what experiences and other things united the freed Israelite slaves as they left Egypt (verses 1-4)? (You might want to check out Exodus 13:21-22; 14:19-22; 16:14-15; 17:5-7.)
- Paul's talk about the Israelites being "baptized into Moses" (verse 2) and drinking from Christ (verse 4) only make sense when we know Paul is telling the Exodus story with *typology*, where one thing is a "type"—a model, a pattern—of something that follows

it later. Why does Paul want his early Christian readers to connect with the Israelites, and how does typology help him make that connection?

- Paul reminds his readers that God judged the people in the wilderness. (You might want to check out Numbers 14:1-25; 21:5-6; 25:1-9.) Why was God angry with the people? What does Paul want his readers to learn from the Israelites' wilderness experience?

- What has happened that makes Paul think he and his readers are those "to whom the end of time has come" (verse 11; see 15:20-28)? How does Paul think this sense of urgency about the future should shape Christian behavior? Do you think Christians two thousand years after Paul's day can share that urgency? Why or why not?

- What kind of caution does Paul urge in verse 12? Has there ever been a time in your life when you've seen what Paul is warning about happen to someone (including, maybe, yourself)? What happened?

- What good news does Paul give people who are facing temptation?

- How do you handle feelings of temptation? What or who has been God's "way out" of temptation for you (verse 13)?

Read and Reflect

Big-Time Bible Blunders

Have you ever noticed a typo in a book you're reading? Did you circle and correct it, or just let it slide?

What would you do if you caught a typo in the *Bible*?

It's happened! In fact, collectors of old and rare books have nicknames for some of history's best-known botched Bibles.

- "The Vinegar Bible"—Published in 1717, the heading on one page calls Jesus' parable of the vineyard (Luke 20:9-19) the "parable of the vinegar."[8] I'm sure the printer felt bitter regret. (Sorry, I couldn't resist.)
- "The Judas Bible"—This 1613 edition mistakenly says, in Matthew 26:36, that *Judas*, not *Jesus*, went with his disciples to Gethsemane.
- "The Wicked Bible"—This 1631 Bible commands readers, in Exodus 20:14, "Thou shalt commit adultery." (Oops!)

You know how your Language Arts teacher is always telling you to proofread your essays? *This is why!*

(On the other hand, typos might pay off. The "Wicked" Bible's printers had to pay a fine and destroy as many copies as they could,[9] so only ten copies are known to still exist. One of the copies, at auction, recently sold for over $47,000.[10])

I wonder whether this session's half truth—"God won't give you more than you can handle"—began as a simple but significant misreading of a Bible verse. It basically misquotes 1 Corinthians 10:13, which says God won't let us *be tempted* beyond our ability to handle *the temptation*. But somewhere along the line, those bits about temptation dropped out. Maybe some first-century Christian youth group was playing a game of "Telephone" with the Apostle Paul's letter; who knows?

Whether somebody skipped a few words or just misunderstood Paul's point, a promise about God's loving faithfulness turned into a very different kind of statement—a "theological typo" that Christians, definitely shouldn't let slide.

Tempting, Isn't It?

Paul was writing to believers in Corinth to clear up some of their questions. They were new to faith in Jesus (of course, in the first century every Christian was) and they faced the disadvantage of trying to follow Jesus faithfully in one of ancient Greece's most famously beautiful but also notoriously sinful cities. All the temples and statues in Corinth honored the gods of Mount Olympus, not the God of Israel, the God and Father of the Lord Jesus. Idol worship ran rampant in Corinth. Its tendrils snaked into so many aspects of everyday life, it was hard to ignore—and all too easy to make moral compromises with.

Food, for example. Want to eat? (Most folks do.) In ancient Corinth, you had to buy your meat in the public marketplace, like everyone else. Trouble was, you had no way of knowing whether the meat you bought came from animal sacrifices to idols. Sure, *you* would know "a false god isn't anything in this world" (1 Corinthians 8:4)—but if you ate meat that was dedicated to false gods, would you somehow be giving a little approval to idol worship? What if a fellow believer who was less mature in faith happened to see you chowing down, and it rattled him so badly he started to waver? In that case, "the weak brother or sister for whom Christ died is destroyed by your knowledge" (8:11). Paul said he'd rather go hungry than give in to the temptation to eat sacrificed meat.

Or consider the fact that sex was a big part of worshiping idols. Having sex with temple prostitutes was a way of communing with the divine; at least, that's what the highly ritualized, super-secretive cults in Corinth taught. Christians knew better—or were supposed to. But some Corinthian Christians were visiting temple prostitutes, a habit that, in some cases, opened the door to more sexual immorality; one man was "having sex with his father's wife" (5:1). Sexual temptations can be hard to resist, but Paul didn't think many in the congregation were even trying.

And so Paul retells the Exodus story to the Corinthians. He reminds them that many of the freed Hebrews abused their freedom to indulge themselves, defying God and grumbling against God's goodness. "God was unhappy with most of them, and they were struck down in the wilderness" (10:5) and never saw the Promised Land. Paul urges his readers to learn from their spiritual ancestors' mistakes and to resist all temptations to ungodly behavior.

What This Half Truth Gets Right: God Knows We Have Limits

That's where the *whole* truth behind this session's half truth comes in. Paul reassures the Corinthians that he's not setting some impossibly high behavioral bar for them. "God is faithful," Paul tells them, and "won't allow you to be tempted beyond your abilities. Instead, with the temptation, God will also supply a way out so that you will be able to endure it" (10:13).

Paul tells the Corinthians the temptations they're wrestling with, as serious as they are, are nothing new. Food, sex, money—these things have always proved potential pitfalls. But Paul's larger point is this: When we feel the most pressure to give up on God, *just then* God refuses to give up on us! God provides a way for us to escape temptation. We have only to look for and take it!

- Maybe we stop to pray when we feel tempted.
- Maybe we remove ourselves from circumstances where temptations are around.
- Maybe we confide in a fellow believer or seek a professional's help.

Whatever form our escape route may take, it's a gift from God.

Although this half truth has forgotten that Paul was talking about temptation, it manages to get God's faithful concern for us right. God doesn't want to watch us crash and burn when we face life's trials. Instead, God promises to help us through them. As God said through the prophet Isaiah, "When you pass through the waters, I will be with you....When you walk through the fire, you won't be scorched..." (43:2).

What This Half Truth Gets Wrong: God Doesn't Pile On

Unfortunately, there's a *major* problem in saying, "God won't give you more than you can handle." The inevitable implication is this: God is giving you tough stuff to deal with in the first place.

At its core, this half truth shares the same flawed premise we saw in the first half truth we looked at, "Everything happens for a reason." As we saw then, while God can certainly *use* anything that happens to us, God doesn't necessarily *cause* everything that happens to us—including our suffering. Scripture is uniquely inspired by God, and we should be careful thinking that our hardships, while very real and very painful, are sent from God.

I believe God doesn't give us more than we can handle because God isn't interested in giving us hardship at all. God doesn't "pile on" when we're having hard times, burdening us until just before we reach our breaking point. God doesn't kick us when we're already down. And, no, God doesn't always, or even usually, take away our hardship with a snap of the divine fingers—but God *does* always bear it with us.

We know this because, in Jesus Christ, we meet a God who, so far from dishing out suffering and heartache and pain, takes it all upon God's own self. Jesus "offered prayers and requests with loud cries and tears as his sacrifices to the one who was able to save him from death" (Hebrews 5:7). Jesus knows firsthand what it feels like to be weighed down and overcome with suffering; even as he was dying on the cross, he called out, "My God, my God, why have you left me?" (Matthew 27:46; Mark 15:34). He wasn't playacting—he felt pain in the depth of his soul just as intense as anyone else who's ever prayed a prayer like that. But if God brought Jesus through the darkness of suffering for the sins of the world to a resurrection morning, how much more can God be trusted to bring *us* through *our* suffering? And so the apostle Peter urges his readers, "Cast all your anxiety on him, because he cares for you" (1 Peter 5:7 NRSV).

God gives us a Savior who strengthens us to cope with pain, confusion, fear, sadness, and trouble. Instead of giving us more than we can handle, God gives us a Savior who can handle it all.

Suggested Activities

1. Build a Weight-Bearing Structure

Using only drinking straws, pipe cleaners, and paper clips, build a structure that can support a golf ball. In order to successfully complete the challenge, you'll have to experiment to find out how much weight various arrangements of your building materials can bear. (If you want inspiration or hints online, try such sites as "Tall Tower Challenge" at https://www.howtosmile.org/resource/smile-000 -000-003-953.) As you work, think about how *you* must not give your structure more than it can handle—but remember (as Adam Hamilton writes in *Half Truths*) that *God* helps us handle all that we are given!

2. Practice *Lectio Divina*

Lectio divina is a Latin phrase that means "divine reading." It is a way of reading Scripture that focuses on making ourselves open and receptive to the way God uses a particular passage to speak directly to us. There is no single "right way" to do *lectio divina*; here is one method you can use:

- Sit in a comfortable and quiet space and read Psalm 27 aloud, making a note of a word, phrase, or image that captures your attention; mark it in your Bible or write it down on another piece of paper. Spend a few minutes simply thinking about what you've noticed.
- Now read the psalm again. Where do you see or hear your life connecting with these words? Write about or draw a picture of this connection.
- Read the psalm a final time. What do you sense God calling you to do or to be today in response to this psalm?

3. Watch a Movie Clip

Watch the scene near the end of *The Lord of the Rings: The Return of the King* (2003) where, as Frodo and Sam are almost at the end of the quest to destroy the evil ring of power, Frodo, exhausted and at his breaking point, decides he can't go on.

- How does Sam become Frodo's "way out" of the temptation to give up?

- How might this scene illustrate how God is with us when we are struggling with burdens of our own?
- How can you "carry" someone who is having trouble enduring difficult times?

4. Write an Encouraging Letter

Paul wrote to the Corinthians when he knew that the congregation was facing temptations. We may not always know when someone is wrestling with a temptation, but we can often observe when someone is going through tough times. Write a brief letter of encouragement to someone you know who is enduring difficult circumstances. (A handwritten letter can communicate a level of personal warmth and concern that e-mails and text messages can't always match.) If possible and appropriate, make an offer of practical help in your letter. Consider quoting an encouraging verse from Scripture.

Daily Bible Readings

Day 1: Isaiah 43:1-4

God spoke these promises through Isaiah to a community—the Jewish exiles living in Babylon—but we can also read them as promises to us as individuals. What deep waters or burning fires have you faced (or are you facing) in your life? Can you sense God's presence with you in those circumstances? How? Why does it matter that God does not say "if" we face such times, but "when"?

Day 2: James 1:13-18

The Apostle James may have felt that he was correcting a "theological typo" for his readers. What truths does he tell them about God's character? What "perfect gifts" has God given you in your life? How do James's words help us when we're facing times of temptation or trouble?

Day 3: Psalm 77

In the first half of this psalm, the psalm-singer certainly feels as though he or she is facing more than one person can handle. What happens so that the second half of the psalm communicates a very different experience? What does this psalm teach us about handling times of sorrow and grief?

Day 4: Hebrews 4:14-16; 5:7-9

How does the truth that Jesus lived a fully human life benefit us when we are being tested or are facing suffering? How confidently do you approach God when you pray? What was a time you found God's grace when you needed help? How did that grace come to you, and how did you respond?

Day 5: 1 Peter 5:6-11

How does remembering that we are not the only people who suffer help us bear suffering? What explanation does Peter give for his readers' suffering? Does it help you make sense of suffering today? Why or why not? What hope does Peter offer his readers?

Day 6: Philippians 4:10-13

What is the Apostle Paul's secret to experiencing contentment in all circumstances? What is something in your life currently for which you need God's strength to help you endure? How can you encourage someone else who needs to endure tough times, as the Philippians encouraged Paul?

4.

GOD SAID IT, I BELIEVE IT, THAT SETTLES IT

Every scripture is inspired by God and is useful for teaching, for showing mistakes, for correcting, and for training character, so that the person who belongs to God can be equipped to do everything that is good.

—2 Timothy 3:16-17

Gather Around God's Word

Make your ways known to me, LORD; teach me your paths.

Lead me in your truth—teach it to me—because you are the God who saves me.

(Psalm 25:4-5)

Open the Bible and light a candle.

God of truth, you have promised that your Word does not return to you empty, but achieves the purpose for which you spoke it. By your Spirit, keep us attentive to your living Word, Jesus Christ, that we may discern and do his will, faithfully and joyfully serving and loving others in his name. Amen.

Sing or read "O Word of God Incarnate" (William W. How, 1862)

Jesus said . . . "You are truly my disciples if you remain faithful to my teaching. Then you will know the truth, and the truth will set you free." (John 8:31-32)

Jesus answered, "I am the way, the truth, and the life. No one comes to the Father except through me." (John 14:6)

Getting Started

What do you think of these quotations from famous people about the Bible?

> I would like so much for all Christians to be able to comprehend "the surpassing worth of knowing Jesus Christ" through the diligent reading of the Word of God, for the sacred text is the nourishment of the soul and the pure and perennial source of the spiritual life of all of us.
>
> —Pope Francis[11]

> [The Bible] is full of interest. It has noble poetry in it; and some clever fables; and some blood-drenched history; and some good morals; and a wealth of obscenity; and upwards of a thousand lies.
>
> —Mark Twain[12]

> [The Bible is] not a book of laws and morals—it's a book of stories, about ordinary, unqualified people doing extraordinary things.
>
> —Madeline L'Engle[13]

> I'm trying to be a Christian and the Bible helps me to remind myself what I'm about.
>
> —Maya Angelou[14]

Study the Scripture

Read 2 Timothy 3.

- Paul's description of what people will be like in "the last days" is rough stuff! (See especially verses 1-5.) How does his advice to avoid such people compare or contrast with Jesus' attitude toward "sinners" in such passages as Mark 2:15-17 or Luke 19:10? Do you think Jesus would agree with Paul's advice to Timothy here? Why or why not?
- Paul also writes that "immature women" will be a particular problem in the last days (verses 6-7). Why does Paul seem to have more to say about the women than the people leading them astray? How do Paul's words here compare or contrast with Paul's teachings in 1 Corinthians 14:33b-35? What about in Galatians 3:27-28? What about Paul's own attitude toward women in working with them as partners in ministry? (He mentions ten such women in Romans 16:1-15, including the deacon Phoebe and the apostle Junia.) Do you sense a tension among these texts and, if so, how do you explain it?
- Who were Jannes and Jambres (2 Timothy 3:8)? What do you make of the fact that their story, clearly known to and regarded as important by Paul and Timothy, is not found in the Old Testament?
- What makes Scripture useful, according to Paul, and for what purposes?
- How have you experienced Scripture's usefulness in one or more of the ways that Paul mentions? How did Scripture help you or someone else do "everything that is good" (2 Timothy 3:17)?
- "Scripture," for Paul, meant what we call the Old Testament. Do you think he would agree that his letters, and the rest of the writings in the New Testament, are also inspired and useful? How do you think the church came to claim that they are?
- Scripture is one tool that Paul tells Timothy to use in order to continue in truth. What other resources does Paul offer?

Read and Reflect

No Cracks About "The Book"?

In an old *Star Trek* episode called "A Piece of the Action," the U.S.S. *Enterprise* boldly goes to a "strange new world" that seems awfully familiar. Captain Kirk and Mr. Spock beam down to a planet where an entire society has patterned itself after Prohibition-era Chicago, ruled by rival, machine gun-wielding mob bosses who fight endless skirmishes over territory.

Watching the episode, we can't help wondering how this culture of gangsters, gamblers, and bootleggers could have developed on a planet thousands of light-years from Earth. The answer, it turns out, is funny. A different earth vessel visited about a century earlier and accidentally left behind a book, *Chicago Mobs of the Twenties*. The planet's natives—"very bright and imitative people," Spock says—adopted this book as a blueprint. Now, a hundred years later, they take its every word as infallible guidance for living, even though it never was intended to be that. The mob bosses even proudly display leather-bound copies on lecterns in their offices. The book has become "The Book," and the planet's people tolerate no questioning of it or speaking against it. "You watch it," one boss cautions Kirk. "The Book tells us how to handle things." Another declares, "I don't want any more cracks about The Book!"[15]

Obviously, "The Book" is a stand-in for the Bible. So is the show simply anti-Scripture? Or is it critiquing how some people read and use—or, perhaps, abuse—the Bible?

In *Half Truths*, Adam Hamilton describes bumper stickers that read, "God said it, I believe it, that settles it." The slogan is a declaration of faith in the Bible's importance and authority. It's meant to affirm Scripture as God's Word. It suggests that the speaker has the final say about the meaning of Scripture and about what Christians should believe and do as a result.

But is the slogan really any of these things? Is it even a biblical sentiment? Or is it as misinformed and misguided as those extraterrestrial mobsters' reverence for "The Book"?

"God Said It"?

The Greek word *biblia* means "books." Though we've brought them together between one set of covers, the books that make up the Bible emerged over thousands of years, from many places. And they are different *kinds* of books: poetry, history, law, letters, even ecstatic visions. If bookstores didn't already have Bible sections, stockers would have a hard time knowing where to shelve this volume.

Parts of Scripture do present themselves as speech from God. The phrase "Thus saith the Lord" shows up over four hundred times in the King James version.[16] But the Bible itself never claims God as its author.

Tradition identifies numerous people as biblical authors: Moses, King David, King Solomon, the four Evangelists, the early apostles. God's people have always understood that Scripture comes from multiple sources. God didn't drop the Bible, fully finished, from heaven. Instead, God used different people, with their different viewpoints and talents—and, yes, their weaknesses and limitations—to write texts that proved themselves, time and again, to be texts through which God continued to communicate with God's people.

In his second letter to Timothy, the Apostle Paul explains God's connection to Scripture this way: "Every scripture is inspired by God..." (3:16). Remember that, for Paul, "scripture" was our Old Testament. Paul certainly believed that he taught and wrote with God-given authority, but he had no way of knowing that later generations of God's people would consider his letters—let alone letters by Peter and John, and the four Gospels, and the book of Revelation—to be Scripture.

Why did Paul's letters come to be considered Scripture? Because later readers recognized that Paul's words, too, were "inspired." *Inspired* means "God-breathed." It's the same action God took with the first human creature: God "blew life's breath" into it, and "[t]he human came to life" (Genesis 2:7). You and I and all people are "inspired" by God—breathed into and made alive—and so, says Paul, is Scripture.

Some religions do claim that God dictated their sacred writings. Muslims, for example, believe the Qur'an is God's direct speech, spoken in Arabic to Muhammad. The Qur'an is translated and read in other languages, but many Muslims who don't already know Arabic learn the language as a religious duty, for then they believe they can read and recite God's exact words.

It's no judgment against Islamic faith to point out that Christians believe the Bible is different. I heard a college professor of religious studies state the contrast accurately and without judgment: "For Muslims, the Word became book. For Christians, the Word became flesh." Christians believe God's Word—God's most direct, most perfect message to humanity—is Jesus.

Does that mean the Bible is "just a book"? Only if we treat it that way. Unless and until we read Scripture in dependence upon God, its words are just ink on the page or pixels on the screen. But when we ask and expect God to inspire our reading and hearing of Scripture, even as God inspired its writing, then we open ourselves to meeting God's living Word, Jesus, through the Bible's written words. In that sense the Bible is indeed "the Word of God"—not God's direct speech written down, but writings that God still reliably uses, as Paul told Timothy, to teach, correct, and train us in faithful living.

What This Half Truth Gets Right:
"I Believe It"

Christians must take the Bible seriously, and this half truth does. It affirms the Bible's authority. Religious scholars frequently classify the world's faiths according to whether they rely on *general revelation* (knowledge about the divine that is self-evident, easily inferred from nature or experience, or otherwise available to everyone) or *special revelation* (knowledge about the divine that depends on a specific, particular person, text, practice, or other source).

We believe that Jesus is God's Word made flesh. We *don't* believe that that was self-evident when he walked the earth—indeed, as the Gospel of John tells us, "his own people didn't welcome him" (1:11). If you want to know who Jesus really was and is, then you must read the Bible. If you want to know about his resurrection on the first Easter, you must read the Bible.

And it's not just Jesus. If you want to know how God saved the people of Israel from slavery in Egypt, you must read the Bible—no clearly explicit reference to the Exodus has yet been found in any other ancient text. Or if you want to know that the God of Israel, the God and Father of Jesus Christ, created the universe, you must read the Bible—science masterfully explains the *what* and *how* of the natural world, but acknowledges it cannot address the *why*.

Christianity is a religion of special revelation, and the Bible is our indispensable record of that revelation. To one degree or other, Christians believe the Bible.

What This Half Truth Gets Wrong:
"That Settles It"

I'll be honest: Even as I typed that last sentence, I could imagine a dozen or more different objections (some of them my own) from a dozen or more different Christians. I imagined some saying, "What do you mean, 'to one degree or other?' You either believe it or you don't; there's no halfway!" I imagined others saying, "Do you mean I have to believe the Bible when it says Joshua made the sun 'stand still,' or that Jonah survived three days after being swallowed by a big fish? How much of this stuff do *I* have to swallow to still be a Christian?"

Even among Christians, then, appealing to the Bible doesn't always "settle" questions. Some Christians believe the Bible is *inerrant*—without any factual mistakes in any of its content, at least in its (now inaccessible) original manuscripts. Others believe the Bible is *infallible*—trustworthy and without fault in its teachings of faith and ethics. Still others hold neither view; they believe and trust some parts of Scripture, but not others.

Whatever we say we believe about the Bible, we all read Scripture selectively. Honestly, how could we not? As we've seen, the Bible is a big book of many books, written by many people over thousands of years. Even though inspired by God, it does not always speak with one voice about every subject God's people have to be concerned about.

And the biblical authors could not even have dreamed of some subjects God's people must think about today. What does the Bible say, for example, about artificial intelligence? Or climate change? Or gun regulations? Nothing directly. But it has lots to say about how human beings should use their God-given creativity, and how humans should exercise the dominion God gave them over creation, and how God's will for human beings is life. Plenty of biblical texts could be (and have been) cited to talk, even debate, about these and other subjects, but they must be *interpreted and applied* if they are to contribute to meaningful conversations.

Meaningful conversation usually happens only in meaningful relationship. A meaningful relationship with God and meaningful relationships with one another are goals of Christian living. The Bible is a means to those ends—an important, even indispensable tool for knowing and loving God and our neighbor. It has not been given to us so we can use it to shut down those with whom we disagree, or to provide quick and easy answers to difficult, complicated questions.

We forget sometimes, because, as those mobsters on *Star Trek* did with "The Book," we bind our Bibles in leather, gild their pages' edges, and make them look as beautiful as possible. But the Bible is a messy book—a wonderfully rich, impressively diverse, spiritually deep, *messy* book! *That's* its real beauty. And its real value lies in the way God has used it, and still uses it, to bring us to Jesus Christ.

Suggested Activities

1. Make a Bible Bookmark

Design and make a bookmark to use in your Bible, or to give someone else for use in theirs. Your bookmark could be as plain as a strip of cardstock decorated with a favorite verse of Scripture and religious symbols, or something fancier, perhaps using ribbons, yarn, or plastic canvas. (Various online craft sites offer instructions and tutorial videos.) Whichever kind you make, be sure it doesn't just sit around looking nice—give it lots of use as you read your Bible!

2. Blow Up a "Bible Balloon"

Choose a Scripture you find particularly inspiring. Using a marker, write its citation—name of the book, chapter, and verse number(s)—on an uninflated balloon. To remember that this Scripture was inspired by God, "inspire" your balloon by blowing it up and hanging it in a prominent place at home or in your youth ministry's meeting space.

3. Watch a Movie Clip

The 1960 film *Inherit the Wind* is a fictionalized version of the "Scopes Monkey Trial," in which a high school biology teacher was charged with violating a Tennessee law that banned the teaching of Darwin's theory of evolution by natural selection. The film is old and in black-and-white but well worth watching, especially the climactic courtroom exchange at about 1:28:27–1:45:49. Henry Drummond, defending the teacher, cross-examines Matthew Brady, who is prosecuting him.

- What does this scene lead you to think or feel?
- What's your opinion of Brady's defense of the Bible as God's Word?
- How would you, from your own beliefs, respond to Drummond's questioning of the Bible?
- Where do you see arguments about interpreting the Bible in today's society?

4. Donate a Bible

However they may differ in reading the Bible, all Christians agree the Bible matters. Sadly, some Christians do not have access to Bibles. Find a reputable ministry that distributes Bibles in this country or overseas—for example, the American Bible Society (www.americanbible.org) or the Gideons (www.gideons .org). Research their work and consider supporting them so that more believers may have what you probably take for granted, a personal copy of the Scriptures.

Daily Bible Readings

Day 1: Psalm 119:105-112

Psalm 119 is the Bible's longest psalm. (You'd never have guessed that, right?) An extended acrostic psalm, it is the devotional fruit of someone who clearly had a passionate love of Scripture. (Remember, for the psalm-singer this would have meant the Torah, the Hebrew Bible's first five books.) How has Scripture been a light for you? What do you do to increase your joy in reading and meditating on the Bible?

Day 2: Isaiah 40:6-8

These verses date from the end of the Babylonian Exile, when God sent the prophet Isaiah to prepare the people for a return to their homeland after decades away. What causes the prophet's initial reluctance to "call out" God's message? What makes the prophet able to overcome this reluctance? What does this promise mean for you?

Day 3: Deuteronomy 23:12-14

In *Half Truths*, Adam Hamilton explains how some late nineteenth-century American Christians used this text to argue against the use of indoor plumbing in church buildings. Do you think all parts of Scripture are equally important or equally relevant to modern life? Why or why not? If so, how do we apply other Scriptures that may seem strange to twenty-first-century readers? If not, how do we tell which parts are more important and which parts are less?

Day 4: John 1:1-5, 14

Whom does the Gospel of John identify as the Word of God? What are the qualities and characteristics of God's Word? Why does it matter that God's Word became a living, breathing person? In what sense, if any, is the Bible also God's Word?

Day 5: John 16:12-15

What is the Holy Spirit's role in revealing more truth to Jesus' followers after Jesus' death and resurrection? How have you experienced the Spirit's revealing more truth to you over time? How does the Spirit's work of continuing revelation relate to the revelation that is recorded in Scripture?

Day 6: John 20:30-31; 21:25

John the Evangelist is open about the fact that his writings don't and couldn't possibly tell us everything there is to know about Jesus. What does John say was his criterion for deciding what to include? What does John's purpose suggest about the primary purpose of Scripture overall?

5.

LOVE THE SINNER, HATE THE SIN

*Why do you see the splinter that's in your brother's or sister's eye,
but don't notice the log in your own eye? How can you say to your
brother or sister, 'Let me take the splinter out of your eye,' when
there's a log in your eye? You deceive yourself! First take the log out
of your eye, and then you'll see clearly to take the splinter out of your
brother's or sister's eye.*

—Matthew 7:3-5

Gather Around God's Word

Make your ways known to me, LORD; teach me your paths.
Lead me in your truth—teach it to me—because you are the God who saves me.

(Psalm 25:4-5)

Open the Bible and light a candle.

God of truth, none of us may dwell in your holy presence except by your amazing grace. May your Spirit always keep us aware of and thankful for your unmerited love toward us, that we may treat all our neighbors with love, remembering that all have sinned and all are saved by Jesus Christ alone. Amen.

Sing or read "Amazing Grace" (John Newton, 1779)

Jesus said … "You are truly my disciples if you remain faithful to my teaching. Then you will know the truth, and the truth will set you free." (John 8:31-32)

Jesus [said], "I am the way, the truth, and the life. No one comes to the Father except through me." (John 14:6)

Getting Started

Read the Scriptures cited below. Each illustrates one of the Seven Deadly Sins (a traditional catalogue of vices, most prevalent in Roman Catholicism, that are referenced by Adam Hamilton in *Half Truths*). Find the name of the sin in the word search and write it next to the corresponding Scripture. (An answer key appears at the end of this chapter—on your honor, no peeking!)

Genesis 4:3-8
Luke 12:15-21
1 Corinthians 11:21-22
2 Samuel 11:2-5
Daniel 4:28-33
Proverbs 24:30-34
1 Kings 21:1-4

```
W P X I C L Z E Q I S J F U A Q H J V O M L
T R G J A J C D W S L V X N N Z H P Y C O B
D I H Y L M T E V E O D G Z O Z F G R G E M
E I X X P V P E B I T H B R Y B H L Y I R P
J O Q U L B U R W X H C W N N E Q G J I D Z
S M X M C Q W G Q W F K M N O B M F T Y G E
G H S Z S B T K M H W M T C T O P W T S U L
W R A T H Y F D R C Y B I L T J B J I E P W
B G O A N Y V L A O M O R I U J V M J B I O
K Y V H B U D G U Q B D M J L C M L J G W K
G Y P D K C I M A Z L E B N G K N I W I X Z
N Q V O S P Y V N E H E I R X R Y N X B M Z
M W P A X D C I M P C R N M S W L E R N K Q
```

Study the Scripture

Read Matthew 7:1-5.

- Why does Jesus say we should not judge others?
- What exaggerated image might Jesus use today, instead of splinters and logs in people's eyes, to make the same point he originally made?
- Does Jesus' warning against passing judgment on others mean we can never say anybody's actions are wrong or sinful? Why or why not?

Read and Reflect

Everyone Else a Sinner?

The last half truth we're looking at in this study reminds me of my favorite church joke. (Well, it's not *actually* my favorite. My actual favorite is about a big, shaggy Saint Bernard who reads the Bible. But that's a different story.)

Pastor John was a preacher whose favorite themes were sin and judgment. Week in and week out, he preached about how terrible the world had become, how angry God was, and how desperately everyone in his congregation needed to shape up and repent!

And week in and week out, as Pastor John's parishioners filed out of worship, one man, Frank, would shake Pastor John's hand, look him square in the eye, and say, "You *sure* told 'em today, Reverend!" Frank never thought anything Pastor John preached about applied to *him*.

Frank's apparent apathy in the face of God's wrath drove Pastor John *crazy*. But Pastor John had made it his personal mission to save Frank's soul. He was determined to preach a sermon that would make it clear that Frank, too, was a sinner.

One winter Sunday, a huge blizzard blew into town. Nobody could make it to church—except Pastor John and Frank. Pastor John saw his big chance and seized it. He preached his most fiery sermon to a congregation of one. He pounded the pulpit and thumped his Bible with all his might. Sweat and tears poured down his face as he appealed to Frank—the only person in the pews—to repent, for the time was at hand!

The sermon ended. Pastor John went to the back of the sanctuary, as always. Frank gathered up his coat, walked up to Pastor John, shook his hand, looked him square in the eye and said: "Well...if they'd 've been here, you *sure* would've told 'em today, Reverend!"

I think the joke perfectly captures the pitfall at the heart of the statement, "Love the sinner, hate the sin." This half truth sounds innocent enough, even theologically correct. What could be wrong with hating sin? Who could argue against loving sinners? But in the end, this half truth encourages us to make the same mistake both Pastor John and Frank make. It encourages us to look at all those sinners out there, conveniently overlooking the sinner who stares at us every time we look in a mirror.

Jesus' Serious Joke

Jesus enjoyed a good joke (whether or not you think my joke falls into that category). I mean, have you ever stopped to imagine what a camel squeezing through a needle's eye would look like (Mark 10:25)? Or do you remember the time Jesus told Peter that he would miraculously find the money they needed to pay their temple tax in a fish's mouth (Matthew 17:24-27)? And a lot of the characters in the stories Jesus told do some pretty funny things. What self-respecting farmer, for example, scatters his seeds willy-nilly, with an equal chance of falling on good soil or stony ground (Mark 4:3-8)?

If you want further proof that Jesus knew the value of laughter, look no further than this session's Scripture focus. Perhaps you've heard this section of Jesus' "Sermon on the Mount" so many times, it's lost its comedic punch. But take a pencil and try to draw the scene Jesus describes: someone trying to pick a tiny splinter out of someone else's eye, all the while oblivious to the wooden two-by-four sticking out of his own (Matthew 7:3-4)!

Go ahead, try to draw it. I'll wait.

Ridiculous, isn't it? I can imagine that Jesus' joke left his original audience in stitches. But, like some of today's best comedians, Jesus used humor to make a serious point. Whenever we are more concerned about people's sins than about the people themselves, we are stepping into dangerous territory.

And with the half truth "Love the sinner, hate the sin," dangerous territory is exactly where we find ourselves.

What This Half Truth Gets Right:
Sin Is Serious

It's not that sin isn't real or doesn't matter. It is, and it does. And Scripture tells us, again and again, to avoid it.

God cautions Cain, "[I]f you don't do the right thing, sin will be waiting at the door, ready to strike! It will entice you, but you must rule over it" (Genesis 4:7). Unfortunately, Cain went on to kill Abel anyway.

- The sages of ancient Israel warn, "The path of the wicked is like deep darkness; they don't know where they will stumble" (Proverbs 4:19).
- "Avoid every kind of evil," writes the Apostle Paul (1 Thessalonians 5:22). It doesn't get much plainer than that.

Paul, in fact, may be the biblical author with the most to say about sin. For Paul, "sin" is more than an individual's "bad deed." Yes, we commit sins, but sin is a spiritual power that enslaves humanity. Sin is a mysterious, corrupting, cosmic influence that none of us can fully resist, no matter how hard we try. We're all like Cain: at one time or another we've been enticed by sin and have fallen into its clutches. "All have sinned and fall short of God's glory," Paul teaches (Romans 3:23)—and the "wages" (the result) of sin, is death (Romans 6:23).

Given this serious situation, can we afford to ignore sin, as Frank in my joke seems to? Or to pretend that whatever anyone wants to do is fine, so long as they're sincere in their desire to do it? Or to treat sin as "no big deal," or to act as though there are no objective standards of right and wrong? Of course not. Sin is toxic. Sin ruins relationships, destroys our well-being, wastes our resources, and offends our pure and holy God.

We should all follow Paul's instructions to his protégé, the young pastor Timothy: to run away from the temptation of sin and instead to "pursue righteousness, holy living, faithfulness, love, endurance, and gentleness" (1 Timothy 6:11).

What This Half Truth Gets Wrong:
Neighbors, Not "Sinners"

The problem with this half truth is standing in judgment on other people as sinners.

Don't misunderstand: everyone is a sinner. But as soon as Paul states this truth in Romans, in his very next breath, he says, "all are treated as righteous freely by [God's] grace because of a ransom that was paid by Christ Jesus" (Romans 3:24). And as soon as Paul claims that the wages of sin is death, he immediately says, "God's gift is eternal life in Christ Jesus our Lord" (6:23).

When it comes to sin and salvation, everyone is on a level playing field. None of us stands a chance against sin on our own. All of us depend on God's saving grace, freely given in Jesus.

That means we can't be like Pastor John in my joke—always accusing, scrutinizing, judging others as sinners so that we can oh so generously love them in spite of their sins. As Adam Hamilton points out in *Half Truths*, not even Jesus ever commanded his followers to "love sinners"—although Jesus did in fact love sinners throughout his earthly ministry. Instead, Jesus commanded, "You must love your neighbor as you love yourself" (Matthew 22:39, quoting Leviticus 19:18).

Do you see the difference? If I approach you as a sinner, I set myself up as better than you. But if I approach you as a neighbor—as a fellow human being who is also loved by God and for whom Jesus also died—then we can have a real relationship. We can see in each other's lives how God's Spirit is constantly at work to make us both holy, as God is holy.

Finally, Adam Hamilton gives us one last thing to think about regarding this half truth. He says he's been hearing Christians talk about "loving the sinner but hating the sin" when they discuss whether the church should welcome people who are homosexual or who are involved in same-sex relationships. Christians disagree about what loving our neighbors who are gay and lesbian looks like— but, as Hamilton says, we all can and should agree on this: "What we can see clearly, and what is unmistakable regarding God's will, is that we love. The truth in 'Love the sinner, hate the sin' stops with the first word: *Love*.[17]

Truth and Love

As we finish our study of half truths that Christians often believe but really shouldn't, I want to leave you with one of the most helpful rules I know for reading Scripture. It's from Augustine of Hippo, an early fifth-century priest and bishop and one of the most influential Christian thinkers the world has seen. In his book *On Christian Doctrine*, Augustine writes:

> Whoever, then, thinks that he understands the Holy Scriptures,
> or any part of them, but puts such an interpretation upon them
> as does not tend to build up [the] twofold love of God and our
> neighbor, does not yet understand them as he ought.[18]

Whenever you hear someone using Scripture in a way that doesn't seem to lead to greater love, be suspicious. Think and pray about what you're hearing. Go back to the actual words in your Bible. Use your God-given intellect and draw on your experience to make up your mind. And remember Augustine's rule: if an interpretation of Scripture doesn't lead us to love God and our neighbor more, it's more than likely a half truth at best.

And be open to having your understanding of Scripture corrected sometimes too. When it comes to loving God and neighbor, we *all* have room for growth. Thanks be to God that God doesn't wait until we've "figured it all out" to love us, to save us, and to begin making us more like Jesus! Now we know only in part; but one day, in God's good time, we will "know completely in the same way that [we] have been completely known" (1 Corinthians 13:12).

Suggested Activities

1. Study Scriptures About Sin

Reread at least one of the Bible passages cited in the word search activity. Now that you know which sin each passage illustrates, what do these passages actually teach about that sin? Using a concordance or an Internet Bible search, what other verses about this sin can you find? How can the sin be recognized? How can God's people flee from the sin? What stories does Scripture contain of people resisting this sin? Where do you see this sin as a threat in today's world or in your own life?

2. Write a Prayer of Confession

The Psalms contain many examples of prayers confessing sin. Psalm 51 is probably the most famous. Tradition tells us that King David wrote and prayed Psalm 51 to confess his sin of lusting after and being with Bathsheba (as well as the sins that flowed from it; read all of 2 Samuel 11 for the full story). After reading Psalm 51, try writing your own prayer of confession. You don't have to write it as a psalm or a poem. You don't even have to use words; your prayer might take the form of a drawing or an abstract design. Whether words or images, communicate not only your sorrow for your sins but also your trust in God's mercy and forgiveness.

3. Make and Share Friendship Bread

In the Bible, the act of "breaking bread," or eating, with someone symbolizes solidarity and community. The positive connotations of eating the same food at the same table with others are one reason Jesus' opponents criticized him as a friend of sinners (Matthew 11:19). The baking and breaking together of Amish friendship bread represents solidarity and community in a unique way, because people usually prepare it from an active starter provided along with the loaf they have been given. Recipes for making the starter and for using it to bake friendship bread are abundant online; one site you may want to visit is the Friendship Bread Kitchen (http://www.friendshipbreadkitchen.com/). Making the bread takes time—ten days, in fact!—but truly loving our neighbors takes time too. Bake and share your bread and also be sure to give a bag of starter so the bread, and the loving community it represents, can continue to spread.

4. Reflect on the Face of Love

In the movie *Dead Man Walking* (1995; rated R for language and mature themes), Susan Sarandon plays Sister Helen Prejean, a real-life nun and advocate for social justice who counsels and forms a bond with convicted killer Matthew Poncelet (played by Sean Penn) before his execution. In the last hour of his life, Matthew finally confesses to his crime. Sister Helen tells him that he has dignity: "You've done terrible things, but you are a son of God." Matthew is overwhelmed; no one has ever called him a son of God. As police guards lead Matthew to the lethal injection chamber, Sister Helen tells him to look at her when he is injected: "I will be the face of love for you." Sister Helen does more than "love the sinner, hate the sin." She recognizes and names Matthew as a fellow sinner, beloved by God and saved by grace, and she embodies that love for Matthew when he needs to feel it most.

God may call few of us to minister as Sister Helen does, but spend some time thinking and praying about these questions:

- Who has been a face of love for you?
- For whom are you—or for whom could you be—the face of God's love today, and how?

Daily Bible Readings

Day 1: Leviticus 19:17-18

Most Christians don't tend to spend much time reading Leviticus, but Jesus, a devout Jew, clearly knew its contents. How do these verses balance the tension between loving people and hating sin? Have you ever rebuked someone for a sin? What happened? What reason does God give for commanding the Israelites to love their neighbors?

Day 2: Psalm 15

If we aren't supposed to think of people as sinners but as neighbors, what do we make of the psalm-singer's statement that "someone who despises those who act wickedly" (verse 4) is fit to dwell on God's holy mountain? Do you think such an attitude has any place in holy living? Why or why not? How did Jesus treat "those who act wickedly?"

Day 3: Proverbs 4

A wise man of ancient Israel teaches his son to avoid the company of sinners. To what extent do you or can you avoid people whose behavior doesn't line up with God's path of wisdom? When, if ever, should Christians cut themselves off from people whose activities can lead them and others to a bad end?

Day 4: Mark 2:14-17

Many Jews in Jesus' day considered tax collectors among the worst of sinners. Tax collectors collaborated with the occupying Roman government, enriching themselves as they gathered money for Caesar's treasury. What defense did Jesus give to critics who questioned why he would eat with tax collectors and other "sinners" (verse 16)?

Day 5: Luke 7:36-50

Why is Simon so offended by Jesus? How does the story that Jesus tells shine light on the real problem in this situation? When have you been challenged to remember God's amazing grace toward you? What extravagant response have you given to God's forgiveness of your sin?

Day 6: Ephesians 4:30–5:2

Have you ever heard Christians angrily shouting at each other about sin, even though Ephesians 4:31 calls us to much different behavior? How do Christians deal with sin in compassionate and forgiving ways, while still taking sin seriously? What is one practical way you will "live in love, as Christ loved us" (5:2 NRSV) as a result of considering the half truths we have studied together?

Answer Key

```
W P X I C L Z E Q I  S  J F U A Q H J V O M L
T R G J A J C  D  W S  L  V X N N Z H  P  Y C O B
D I H Y L M T  E  V E  O  D G Z O Z F G  R  G E M
E I X X P V P  E  B I  T  H B R  Y  B H L Y I  R  P
J O Q U L B U  R  W X  H  C W N  N  E Q G J I  D  Z
S M X M C Q W  G  Q W F K M N  O  B M F T Y G  E
G H S Z S B T K M H W M T C  T  O P W  T S U L
W R A T H  Y F D R C Y B I L  T  J B J I E P W
B G O A N Y V L A O M O R I  U  J V M J B I O
K Y V H B U D G U Q B D M J  L  C M L J G W K
G Y P D K C I M A Z L E B N  G  K N I W I X Z
N Q V O S P  Y V N E  H E I R X R Y N X B M Z
M W P A X D C I M P C R N M S W L E R N K Q
```

NOTES

1. The Heidelberg Catechism (1563), Lord's Day 9/Q&A 26; https://www
   .crcna.org/welcome/beliefs/confessions/heidelberg-catechism. © 2011, Faith
   Alive Christian Resources. This translation approved by Synod 2011 of the
   Christian Reformed Church in North America and by General Synod 2011 of
   the Reformed Church in America.

2. See George Barna, *Real Teens: A Contemporary Snapshot of Youth Culture*
   (Ventura, CA: Gospel Light Publications, 2001), 125.

3. See http://www.britannica.com/topic/Poor-Richard.

4. Joseph Stromberg, "Starving Settlers in Jamestown Colony Resorted to
   Cannibalism," Smithsonian.com, April 30, 2013; http://www.smithsonianmag
   .com/history/starving-settlers-in-jamestown-colony-resorted-to
   -cannibalism-46000815/?no-ist.

5. See Dennis Montgomery, "Captain John Smith," *Colonial Williamsburg
   Journal* (Spring 1994): http://www.history.org/foundation/journal/smith.cfm.

6. Dr. Seuss, *Oh, the Places You'll Go!* (New York: Random House, 1990), 25.

7. *The Confession of 1967* (Presbyterian Church (U.S.A.)), I.B http://www.creeds
   .net/reformed/conf67.htm.

8. See Justin Shatwell, "The Theft of the Vinegar Bible," *Yankee Magazine*, "The
   Yankee Historian" blog, December 2015; http://www.yankeemagazine.com
   /yankee-historian/the-theft-of-the-vinegar-bible#_;

9. See Abby Ohlheiser, "When 'Jesus' was 'Judas' and other pretty stupendous
   Bible typos," *The Washington Post*, February 10, 2015; https://www
   .washingtonpost.com/news/arts-and-entertainment/wp/2015/02/10
   /when-jesus-was-judas-and-other-pretty-stupendous-bible-typos/.

10. https://www.bonhams.com/auctions/22715/lot/5/.

11. Quoted in American Bible Society blog, http://news.americanbible.org/blog /entry/corporate-blog/6-pope-francis-quotes-about-the-bible.

12. *Letters from the Earth*; http://www.twainquotes.com/Bible.html.

13. Heather Webb, "A Conversation with Madeline L'Engle," *Mars Hill Review* 4 (Winter/Spring 1996): 51–65; http://www.leaderu.com/marshill/mhr04 /lengle1.html.

14. Quoted in Morgan Lee, "Seven Quotes Showing Maya Angelou's Love of the Bible and Faith," May 28, 2014; http://www.christianpost.com/news /seven-quotes-showing-maya-angelous-love-of-the-bible-and-faith-120493 /#mf54J1AOVW5qvIVQ.99.

15. *Star Trek*, "A Piece of the Action," teleplay by David P. Harmon and Gene L. Coon, originally aired January 12, 1968. http://www.imdb.com/title /tt0708412/?ref_=fn_al_tt_5.

16. From Blue Letter Bible, http://bit.ly/1mdUid2.

17. Adam Hamilton, *Half Truths* (Nashville: Abingdon Press, 2016), 162.

18. Augustine, *On Christian Doctrine*, chap. 36; http://www.newadvent.org /fathers/12021.htm.

CPSIA information can be obtained
at www.ICGtesting.com
Printed in the USA
LVOW12s0549060516

486923LV00007B/7/P

OXFORD SUBURBS & VILLAGES

THROUGH TIME

ST GILES, HEADINGTON, ST CLEMENTS, COWLEY, IFFLEY, WYTHAM

Stanley C. Jenkins

AMBERLEY PUBLISHING

Victorian Villas in North Oxford

An archetypal North Oxford scene, showing a row of Victorian villas at the west end of Rawlinson Road. These relatively large houses were designed and built for upper middle-class occupants.

First published 2013

Amberley Publishing
The Hill, Stroud, Gloucestershire, GL5 4EP
www.amberley-books.com

Copyright © Stanley C. Jenkins, 2013

The right of Stanley C. Jenkins to be identified as the
Author of this work has been asserted in accordance with
the Copyrights, Designs and Patents Act 1988.

ISBN 978 1 4456 1287 4 (print)
ISBN 978 1 4456 1308 6 (ebook)

British Library Cataloguing in Publication Data.
A catalogue record for this book is available from the
British Library.

Typesetting by Amberley Publishing.
Printed in Great Britain.

Introduction

Oxford originated in the early tenth century as one of the fortified 'burghs' constructed by King Alfred and his descendants during the Viking wars. The new town, which was built on the site of a small, pre-existing settlement, was protected by an encircling wall, which would later delineate the limits of the city centre.

The Domesday Book reveals that the first suburbs had appeared beyond the wall by 1086, when Oxford contained 'as well within the wall as without ... 243 houses which pay geld, and besides these there are 500 houses less 22 so wasted and destroyed that they cannot pay geld'. St Clements was the most important of these early suburbs; it was situated just outside the South Gate, and was in existence by the eleventh century. Archaeological evidence suggests that there may have been similar Anglo-Saxon suburbs beyond the North and West Gates; the area in front of the North Gate known as St Giles had certainly appeared by the twelfth century.

Urban expansion took place steadily throughout the medieval period and by 1801, Oxford had a population of 11,694. Thereafter, the city's population began to expand more rapidly, rising to 23,834 in 1841 and 37,057 by 1901 – much of this growth having taken place in new suburbs that had appeared well beyond the confines of the original urban centre.

The upper sections of the middle class had, for many years, been keen to emulate the lifestyle of the country gentry, and these aspirations became much more pronounced as the industrial revolution got fully into its stride. Successful traders and professional people started to migrate towards the outskirts of the city in considerable numbers; by the 1850s, for example, there were said to be twenty-three 'gentlemen's houses' in the village of Iffley.

The individuals who resided in these country retreats had no intention of creating new suburbs, but as the demand for out-of-town properties increased, powerful landowners such as the Oxford colleges began to plan ambitious residential developments as a means of increasing the value of their land. St John's College, in particular, was instrumental in laying out the Norham Gardens Estate and other areas of North Oxford, which became classic upper middle-class suburbs.

In addition to these prosperous middle-class residential areas, North Oxford contained several working-class enclaves, notably the district of high-density terraced housing known as 'Jericho', and the much later suburban developments in and around Summertown.

Meanwhile, suburban encroachment was taking place elsewhere in the Oxford area, notably around Headington and Cowley. However, the period of greatest expansion in south and east Oxford occurred during the twentieth century, following the establishment of the Morris Motors Works and the neighbouring Pressed Steel factory; the two plants employed around 7,000 people by the mid-1930s, rising to 20,000 in the 1970s.

The growth of the city was accompanied by various boundary changes as the new suburbs and former rural villages were absorbed; St Clements parish, for example, was incorporated into the City of Oxford in 1835 under the provisions of the Municipal Corporations Act, while Headington, Cowley and Iffley were swallowed up during the twentieth century. Meanwhile, a similar process was taking place to the west of Oxford, where several parishes and districts that had formerly belonged to Berkshire were absorbed into the city.

The following chapters are arranged on a geographical basis, Chapter One being a relatively detailed study of the purpose-built Victorian suburbs of North Oxford, while Chapter Two covers the 'absorbed' villages of Headington and Marston. Chapter Three examines St Clements, Cowley Road, Iffley Road and Cowley, and the final chapter looks at a number of villages on the east and west sides of the city.

Some of these Oxford villages, including Iffley, Kennington, Hinksey and Wolvercote, have been joined to Oxford by ribbon development and have in this way been absorbed into the urban area, although Iffley and Wolvercote have nevertheless retained the character of historic villages. Beckley, Cumnor, Forest Hill, Godstow, Horspath, Wytham and Woodeaton, on the other hand, are still surrounded by open countryside, and have remained more or less rural in character.

Acknowledgements

Thanks are due to the Soldiers of Oxfordshire Trust for the supply of photographs on pages 48, 62, 63, 64, 65 and 66. Other images were obtained from the Witney & District Museum, and from the author's own collection.

Above and Opposite: **Victorian Houses in South Oxford**
Terraced houses such as these examples in Chester Street would have appealed to members of the lower middle class, such as bank clerks, shopkeepers and small tradesmen.

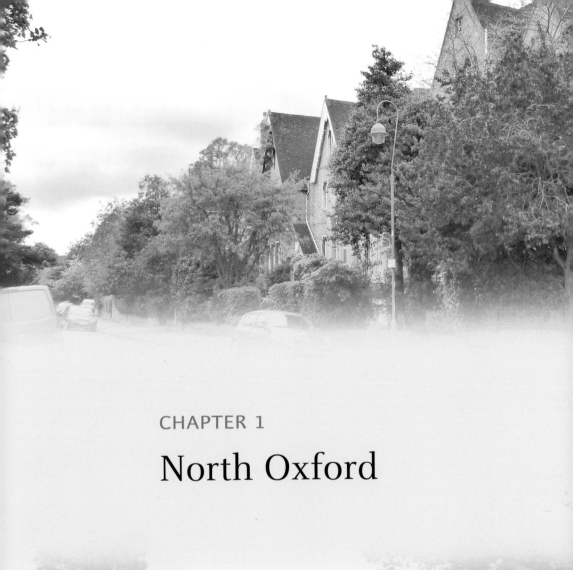

CHAPTER 1

North Oxford

St Giles

Situated immediately to the north of the city wall, St Giles was one of Oxford's first 'suburbs'. The upper view, from a colour-tinted Edwardian postcard, shows the north end of St Giles, looking northwards along the Woodstock Road, with Banbury Road visible on the extreme right. The lower view is looking along the Woodstock Road from a similar position in May 2013; the embattled tower of St Giles' parish church can be seen to the right of the picture.

St Giles' Church

Nestling in the 'V' of the diverging Woodstock and Banbury roads, St Giles' church retains much of the atmosphere of a rural church, which it once was. The building, which consists of a nave, aisles, chancel, west tower and south porch, dates mainly from the thirteenth century, although blocked Norman windows can be seen in the nave. The sepia view shows the church from the east, possibly during the 1940s, while the colour photograph was taken from the south-west in May 2013.

The War Memorial

Standing on a prominent site near St Giles' church, Oxford's war memorial was unveiled in 1921. It is in the form of a fifteenth-century cross upon an octagonal pedestal, and was designed by Thomas Rayson (1888–1976), in association with John Thorpe and Gilbert Gardner. Rayson, who had been involved with the construction of Witney Aerodrome during the Great War, designed similar memorial crosses at Witney, Woodstock and Chester. The accompanying photographs show the memorial during the 1920s, and in 2013.

The Woodstock Road & Banbury Roads

These two roads, which extend northwards from St Giles for a distance of over 2 miles, are synonymous with North Oxford. They are linked by a network of inter-connecting roads which follow an approximate east-to-west alignment, thereby creating an informal 'grid' pattern – although the resulting layout is by no means as regular as that found in many American cities. The upper view shows an electro-diesel bus in Banbury Road, while the lower picture shows typical North Oxford houses in the Woodstock Road.

Mansfield College

Several of Oxford's younger colleges are situated in the North Oxford area, one of these being Mansfield College, which is sited in Mansfield Road, to the east of St Giles. This college originated in Birmingham as a Nonconformist training college, but it moved to Oxford in 1886. The buildings, designed by Basil Champneys (1842–1935), are in traditional medieval style, as shown in the accompanying photographs; the sepia view is an old postcard, while the colour photograph was taken in 2013.

Somerville College

Women were first admitted to Oxford in the 1870s, but they were not allowed to become members of the university until 1920. Lady Margaret Hall and Somerville, the first ladies' colleges, were founded in 1879 as hostels for Anglican and Nonconformist students respectively, but they both became full colleges in 1960. Men were first admitted as undergraduates in 1994. The sepia postcard view is looking westwards across the middle quadrangle (now known as the 'Traffic Quad'), while the recent photograph shows the college entrance.

St Hugh's College

Founded in 1886 by Elizabeth Wordsworth (1840–1932), the first principal of Lady Margaret Hall, St Hugh's College, in St Margarets Road, was intended to cater for clergymen's daughters and others who could not afford the fees at the other ladies' colleges; male students were first admitted in 1986. The college boasts some surprisingly grand buildings in the Queen Anne' style, as shown in this *c.* 1950s sepia postcard view, and in a recent photograph of the main entrance, which was taken in 2013.

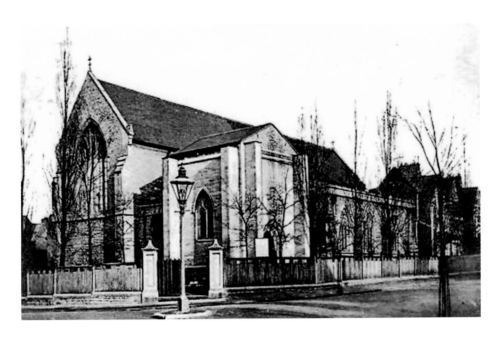

St Margaret's Church

Situated in St Margaret's Road, St Margaret's church was designed by Harry Drinkwater (1844–95). The foundation stone was laid on 8 May 1883 but construction was a protracted business, and although plans for a tower-porch were drawn up by George Frederick Bodley (1827–1907), the tower was never completed. The church was, at first, a chapel of ease within the parish of St Philip and St James, but it became a separate parish in 1896. The upper view is from *c.* 1912, while the lower photograph was taken in 2012.

The Church of St Philip & St James

The upper view provides a further glimpse of St Margaret's church in December 2012; the unfinished tower can be seen on the extreme left. If completed, the tower would have been 88 feet high. The lower photograph depicts the neighbouring church of St Philip & St James in Woodstock Road. Designed by George Edmund Street (1824–81), the diocesan architect, this impressive building was intended to serve as the parish church for the inhabitants of rapidly-expanding North Oxford. The foundation stone was laid on 1 May 1860 and this substantially-built Victorian church was consecrated by the Bishop of Oxford on 8 May 1862.

The parish of St Philip & St James was reunited with the parish of St Margaret in 1976, and the church of St Philip & St James was finally declared redundant in April 1982. It is now the home of the Oxford Centre for Mission Studies.

St Barnabas Church

The suburb of Jericho is an area of closely-spaced Victorian terraced houses that once housed manual workers employed in local businesses such as the Oxford University Press and the Eagle Ironworks. It is situated between Walton Street and the Oxford Canal, and is thought to have derived its name from a long-established inn known as the Jericho House. St Barnabas church was built to serve this populous community. Designed by Sir Arthur Blomfield (1829–99), this remarkable Victorian church was consecrated by the Bishop of Oxford on 19 October 1869. The building is constructed of cement-rendered rubble walling, the overall effect being, in many ways, reminiscent of the late Roman or Byzantine style. The upper view shows the church from Cardigan Street, while the lower photograph was taken from Nelson Street in 2012.

St Barnabas Church

Above: An interior view of the church, possibly dating from the late Victorian period, before the application of coloured decoration on the north wall of the nave. *Below*: This recent photograph, taken in December 2012, shows the cement-rendered exterior walls of the church, which are enlivened by horizontal bands of brickwork. The lofty campanile-type tower originally sported a pyramidal roof cap, but this was removed in 1965, and in its present, slightly truncated form, the tower has a height of 115 feet. *Inset:* The mural panels on the north wall, which illustrate the *Te Deum*, were completed around 1911.

St Aloysius Church

This Roman Catholic church was designed by Joseph Aloysius Hansom (1803–82), the designer of the Hansom cab, and consecrated in 1875. It is constructed of yellow brick, and incorporates a nave, aisles, an apsidal chancel and several side chapels. The church is associated with the Jesuit poet Gerald Manley Hopkins (1844–89), who served as curate here for a period of ten months in 1878.

The upper view shows the interior of the church around 1912, while the colour photograph was taken in 2013. The church is dedicated to Aloysius Gonzaga (1568–91), an Italian nobleman who became a Jesuit, and died of fever while attending to the sick during an outbreak of the plague. The unusual reredos, which can be seen in the interior view and was completed in 1887, has sixty-two statues, the upper tier representing English saints and martyrs, while the lower tier represents the rest of the Catholic Church.

Plantation Road: West End

Running from east to west between Woodstock Road and Kingston Road, Plantation Road was laid out in the 1830s on the alignment of two earlier country lanes. The upper view shows the western end of the road around 1912, while the colour photograph, taken in December 2012, shows No. 39, The Gardener's Arms public house, which is situated in the middle part of the road at the junction of Leckford Place and St Bernard's Road.

Plantation Road: East End

As its name implies, Plantation Road once gave access to an area of land used as nursery gardens, and the road retains much of its rural character. The upper view is looking east along the narrowest part of the road, the Cotswold-stone building visible to the right being a former bakery. The lower photograph is looking in the opposite direction from a position slightly further to the east; the brick house to the left of the picture is No. 30 Plantation Road, which adjoins the old bakery.

Portland Road

Portland Road, which extends eastwards from the Banbury Road, was laid out during the early years of the twentieth century as part of an urban development scheme that was being promoted by Francis Twining (1848–1929), a local businessman who later became Mayor of Oxford. Gothic architecture was no longer fashionable during the Edwardian period, and the houses in Portland Road reflect the 'vernacular revival' style, with bay windows and 'Tudor' gables, as shown in the accompanying illustrations.

Junction of Woodstock Road & Davenant Road

The upper picture shows the north end of Woodstock Road, *c.* 1912, the country lane leading off to the right being Davenant Road. The lower view, taken from a similar vantage point just over a century later, reveals that the scene has now been totally transformed, many more houses having appeared, while the flow of traffic on the busy Woodstock Road is incessant. The road has been widened and partially straightened, but the raised footpath that can be seen to the left in the earlier picture is still in place.

William Wilkinson & The Norham Manor Estate

Laid out by the Witney architect William Wilkinson (1819–1901) on land owned by St John's College, the Norham Manor Estate was built in the 1860s as a residential suburb for wealthy tradesmen and professional people. Wilkinson designed several of the villas himself, while in his role as superintending architect he was able to ensure uniform standards throughout the new estate. Most of the houses were of red or yellow brick construction with prominent stone dressings.

Wilkinson subsequently published a book entitled *English Country Houses* containing plans and drawings of recently-erected domestic properties, one of these being No. 13 Norham Gardens, a 'show-piece' villa on the Norham Manor Estate, which is shown above. The accompanying ground plan reveals that, in addition to the dining room, conservatory and lobby, the accommodation included a library and servants' hall, the implication being that a house of this size would require perhaps half a dozen servants.

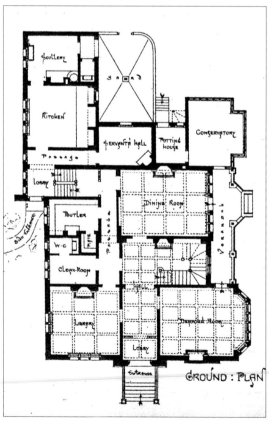

GROUND : PLAN

No. 13 Norham Gardens

This illustration from *English Country Houses* shows No. 13 Norham Gardens from the south-west – the drawing room, dining room and conservatory faced south to ensure maximum sunlight. On 16 October 1869, *Jackson's Oxford Journal* reported that this residence, which was being built for Thomas Dallin MA, a Fellow of Queen's College, was 'the largest on the estate', and the work 'was being carried out in a very substantial manner, with red brick faced with light-coloured stone'.

No. 13 later became the home of Canadian physician William Osler (1849–1919), a Fellow of Christ Church and Regius Professor of Medicine at Oxford, and his American wife, Grace Renée. The Oslers enlarged the house and altered its appearance; the 1911 census reveals that they had five live-in servants, including a butler, cook and maids. The lower view is a first-floor plan of No. 13 as originally constructed; note that separate stairs were provided for the servants.

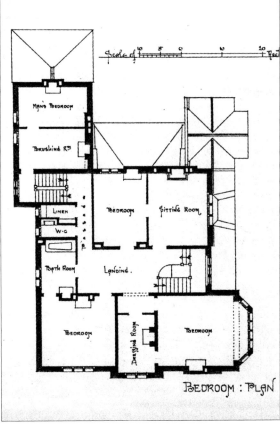

23

No. 9 Norham Gardens

Above: No. 9 Norham Gardens was designed by Charles Buckeridge (1832–73) and built in 1868, the first occupant being Montagu Burrows, the Regius Professor of Modern History. The building is of red-brick construction, with a steeply-pitched roof profile and prominent half-hipped gables that give it a slightly French appearance. *Below*: The drawing room of a mid-Victorian villa, as envisaged by William Wilkinson in his book *English Country Houses*. Wall-mounted candles appear to be the only form of lighting.

No. 3 Norham Gardens

Above: No. 3 Norham Gardens was also designed by Charles Buckeridge. Built in 1868 for Henry Hammons, a bookseller, the house is of yellow brickwork, with distinctive fenestration and an unusual 'stepped' porch. *Below*: The master bedroom of a typical Victorian house, as portrayed in *English Country Houses*. The dressing table is situated in the bay window, while a washstand with matching 'his' and 'hers' water jugs can be seen behind the bed.

The Walton Manor Estate – No. 113 Woodstock Road

The Walton Manor Estate was slightly earlier than the Norham Gardens Estate. In 1859, St John's College set up a committee to consider how an area of college land to the west of the Woodstock Road could be profitably developed. Samuel Seckham was selected as the first architect, but he was subsequently replaced by William Wilkinson, who designed a number of the new houses including No. 113 Woodstock Road, shown above, which was built in 1863 for Edwin Butler, a wine merchant. Victorian architecture was despised by mid-twentieth-century town planners and their friends in the architectural establishment, and in these circumstances many of the large North Oxford houses were threatened with destruction, one of the victims being No. 113, which was demolished in the 1960s. Its site is now occupied by a modern development known as 'Butler Close', which is shown in the lower illustration. *Inset*: A recent view showing Butler Close from the Woodstock Road.

No. 60 Banbury Road

No. 60 Banbury Road, at one time known as 'Shrublands', was another typical North Oxford villa; it was designed by William Wilkinson and the first occupant was Thomas George Cousins, the proprietor of a chemist's shop in Magdalen Street. The house is of yellow-brick construction with Bath stone dressings, and when first built in 1869 it contained three reception rooms, five bedrooms and a conservatory, as well as a kitchen, cellars and other service rooms.

Study of the accompanying ground plan will reveal that, as is usual with Wilkinson's villas, the kitchen, scullery, larder and other service rooms were laid out in such a way that the servants could go about their daily work without impinging unnecessarily upon the master or his family – a servants' passage being provided alongside the main hallway.

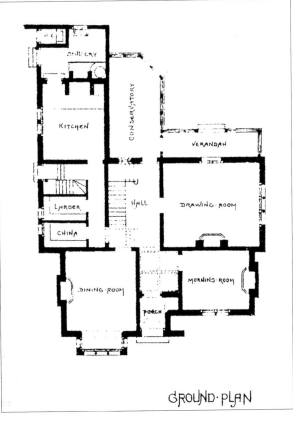

GROUND·PLAN

No. 60 Banbury Road & No. 82 Woodstock Road

Above: A recent view of No. 60 Banbury Road, which is now an integral part of Kellogg College, a constituent college of the University of Oxford; the elaborate finials have been removed, but the building is otherwise in excellent condition. *Below*: Completed in 1887, No. 82 Woodstock Road was designed by William Wilkinson in conjunction with his nephew, Harry Wilkinson Moore (1850–1915), the two architects having formed a partnership in 1881. William Wilkinson retired in 1886 and, thereafter, his nephew worked alone.

No. 31 Banbury Road

Built in 1866 for George Ward, No. 31 Banbury Road was another example of William Wilkinson's characteristic North Oxford villa designs. On 13 October 1866 *Jackson's Oxford Journal* opined that 'handsome villas' of this kind 'materially contribute to the appearance of the locality'. In a previous edition, the same journal had mentioned that Mr Wilkinson's villas were all equipped with 'Moule's patent earth closets, with self-activating floor apparatus'. The tall window that can be seen to the left of the front door provided ample light for the main stairway, while the oriel window to its left illuminated the bathroom. Sadly, No. 31 was demolished in the 1960s, and its site is now occupied by modern buildings.

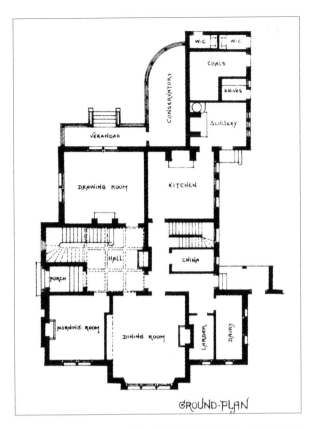

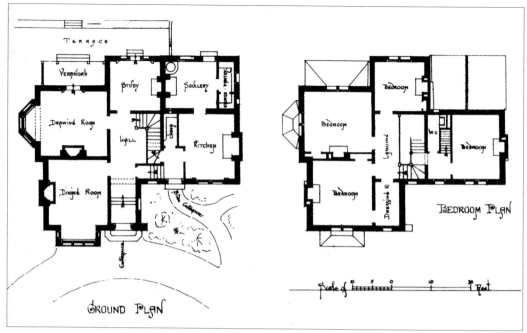

TERRACE

VERANDAH | STUDY | SCULLERY

DRAWING ROOM

HALL | KITCHEN

DINING ROOM

GROUND PLAN

BEDROOM

BEDROOM | W.C

BEDROOM

BEDROOM

Dressing R.

BEDROOM PLAN

Scale of Feet

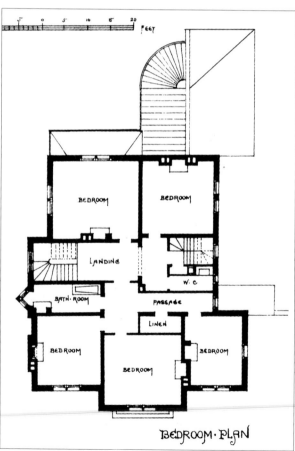

FEET

BEDROOM | BEDROOM

LANDING

W.C

BATH·ROOM | PASSAGE

LINEN

BEDROOM | BEDROOM

BEDROOM

BEDROOM·PLAN

Some Additional House Plans
Above: The floor plans of Edwin Butler's house at No. 113 Woodstock Road (*see page 26*) were published in *English Country Houses*. The ground floor incorporated two reception rooms and a 'study', together with the kitchen and service area, which were entirely separate from the 'family' rooms. This layout was echoed on the upper floor, which contained three main family bedrooms and a servants' bedroom above the kitchen. *Left*: The upper floor of No. 31 Banbury Road provided sufficient space for four 'family' bedrooms and a fifth bedroom for live-in servants; the bathroom on the top of the landing was intended for 'family' use, while the WC at the top of the 'back stairs' was presumably intended for the servants. On a footnote, it is often claimed that these mid-Victorian villas were built to accommodate 'married dons', though in reality this is incorrect, as dons were not allowed to marry during the mid-Victorian period.

Wychwood & Summerfields Schools

Above: Founded in 1897 by Margaret Lucy Lee (1871–1955), daughter of the vicar of Leafield, and her friend Annie Sophia Batty (*d.* 1934), the Wychwood School moved to No. 74 Banbury Road in 1918, and it later acquired No. 72. These two large villas dated from 1885, and both had been designed by Messrs Wilkinson & Moore. It is seen here in 2012. *Below*: Summerfields School, *c.* 1928, about three quarters of a mile to the north, was founded as a Boys' Preparatory School in 1864 by Archibald and Gertrude Maclaren.

No. 217 Woodstock Road & No. 22 Museum Road

Above: No. 217 Woodstock Road was one of a pair of villas erected in 1900. Gothic architecture had gone out of fashion by the end of the Victorian period, and early twentieth-century houses tended to exhibit 'vernacular revival' features, such as tile-hung bay windows and 'Tudor' style timber-framing. The first occupant of No. 217 was Mrs Frances Richardson, the wife of a clergyman. *Left*: No. 22 Museum Road and the neighbouring properties were erected in 1873 as a speculative venture by John Dorn, a local builder. The most noteworthy occupant of No. 22 was perhaps Frederick Gaspard Brabant (1856–1929), a writer, teacher and private tutor who, as an undergraduate, had 'attained the rare distinction of adding a first in mathematical moderations to two firsts in classics'. He was also an enthusiastic local historian, who produced a number of informative guide books about Oxfordshire, Berkshire, Sussex, North Wales and the Lake District.

CHAPTER 2

Headington & East Oxford

Headington Road & Bridge

In 1852, Gardner's *History, Gazetteer & Directory of the County of Oxford*, described 'the High road from Oxford to Headington' as 'broad and steep', with 'a fine terrace walk constructed by the general subscription of the University'. Hereabouts, according to legend, an Oxford student had once been attacked by a wild boar from Shotover Woods, but he 'escaped by cramming a volume of Aristotle down the throat of the savage beast'!

In 1824, a palatial house known as Headington Hill Hall was erected for the Morrell family, proprietors of Morrell's Brewery, and as the Morrell's land eventually extended over both sides of the road, William Wilkinson was asked to design an ornamental footbridge, which was built in 1866 and now forms a prominent local landmark. The old postcard view is looking east towards Headington around 1912, and the colour photograph was taken in June 2013.

The Britannia at New Headington

Headington Road, which continues eastwards as 'London Road', now forms part of the A420 – a major thoroughfare for traffic heading into and out of Oxford. The upper view shows the Britannia Inn on the corner of London Road and Lime Walk around 1912. The scene is still semi-rural in character, although urban expansion was, by that time, well under way in nearby streets such as Windmill Road and Lime Walk. The colour photograph was taken from a similar position in 2012.

London Road, New Headington

Above: A general view of London Road, looking east around 1930. The Headington area was once entirely rural but, according to the 1933 *Little Guide to Oxford*, the original village had, by that time, become 'quite overshadowed by the large new suburb of Oxford, which includes, besides Headington, Highfield and Headington Quarry'. *Below*: A recent view of London Road in June 2013. The road junction visible in the distance gives access to Windmill Road and Old High Street.

Lime Walk, New Headington

Above: An early twentieth-century postcard view of Lime Walk, looking north towards London Road, with the red-brick façade of the newly-built All Saints church visible to the right. The corner shop that can be seen to the left of the picture was a post office and grocer's shop. *Below*: A recent view, taken from a position slightly further to the south in June 2013. Headington was incorporated into the City of Oxford in 1929.

All Saints Church, New Headington

A closer view of All Saints church, which was designed by Arthur Blomfield & Son and consecrated on 29 May 1910. This new church was intended to cater for the growing district of New Headington, which had hitherto been served by a corrugated-iron mission church in Perrin Street. As originally built, the church consisted of a nave, side-aisles and a west porch, but a chancel was added in 1935. The upper view dates from around 1912, while the recent photograph was taken in 2013.

All Saints Church, Highfield, Headington.

John Wesley Woodward

A postcard view showing the rather bleak, bare-brick interior of All Saints church before the addition of the chancel. A plaque within the church commemorates John Wesley Woodward (1879–1912) of No. 2 Windmill Road, Headington, a cellist and member of the *Titanic*'s orchestra who, with his fellow musicians, played ragtime and other popular melodies as the great liner sank by the bows; most witnesses agree that, at the very end, the band played *Nearer My God to Thee*. The memorial plaque, which is difficult to photograph, is inscribed with the following words:

TO THE GLORY OF GOD AND IN
MEMORY OF
JOHN WESLEY WOODWARD
BANDSMAN ON THE S.S. *TITANIC*
WHO WITH HIS COMRADES
NOBLY PERFORMED HIS DUTY TO
THE LAST
WHEN THE SHIP SANK
AFTER COLLISION WITH AN
ICEBERG
ON APRIL 15 1912.
BORN SEPT 11, 1879.
'NEARER MY GOD TO THEE.'

St Andrew's Church, Old Headington

Old Headington, which is linked to New Headington by Old High Street and Ostler Road, retains the atmosphere of a rural village, in spite of suburban encroachments during the nineteenth and twentieth centuries. The parish church, originally Norman, was enlarged at various times, and in its present form the building incorporates a nave, aisles, chancel, south porch and an embattled west tower. The upper view shows the church around 1912, while the colour photograph was taken in June 2013.

Thatched Cottages in Old Headington

This postcard view of Headington village, dating from around 1910, depicts a row of old thatched cottages at the west end of St Andrew's Road. Sadly, these traditional stone buildings were demolished in the 1930s and a row of modern houses, designed by Ronald Fielding Dodd, was erected in their place. The lower picture, taken in 2013, shows the replacement buildings, which are numbered from 27 to 33. Their continuous frontage maintains the profile of the demolished cottages, but they are set further back from the street.

St Andrew's House, Old Headington

The substantial Victorian building known as St Andrew's House is situated in Old Headington, at the corner of St Andrew's Road and Osler Road. It is of Cotswold-stone construction, and served as a vicarage from 1881 until 1977. The upper view shows the building during the early years of the twentieth century, while the colour view was taken over a century later in June 2013. The house is partially hidden by a large tree, although the Osler Road frontage can be clearly seen.

Old Headington Village

Above: A colour-tinted postcard view of Old Headington village, looking southwards along Old High Street around 1912. The large building that can be seen in the distance is a former farmhouse known as Linden House, which was substantially rebuilt during the Victorian period. *Below*: This recent view reveals that several old cottages have been replaced, but Linden House – now The Priory – has survived; it was purchased by a community of Dominican Sisters in 1923, and acquired by the Congregation of the Sacred Heart in 1968.

St Nicholas Church, Old Marston

Marston, to the north-west of Headington, consists of the suburb of New Marston and the original Old Marston village, which were absorbed into Oxford in 1929 and 1991 respectively. The upper view shows Old Marston parish church, which consists of a nave, aisles, chancel, south porch and west tower. Although the exterior details of the church reflect the Perpendicular style, the nave arcades and chancel arch are Early English. The photographs were taken *c.* 1920 and in June 2013.

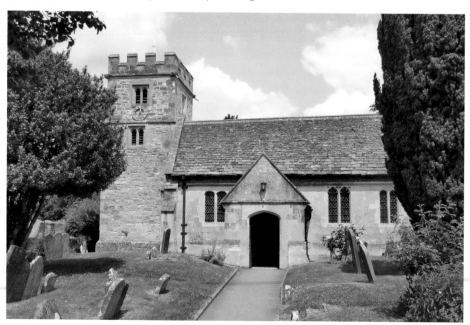

Cromwell's House, Marston

This seventeenth-century house in Old Marston was the home of Unton Coke, a leading Parliamentarian during the Civil War, and it is said to have been the headquarters of the New Model Army during the siege of Oxford – negotiations leading to the formal surrender of the city were held here in May 1646, and the Royalist garrison finally capitulated on 20 June. The upper picture shows Cromwell's House and neighbouring buildings around 1912, while the recent view was taken in 2013.

CHAPTER 3

St Clement's, Cowley & South Oxford

St Clement's & The Plain

St Clement's, one of Oxford's earliest suburbs, originated in the tenth century, when a *brycggesett*, or 'bridge-settlement', grew up on the east side of the River Cherwell. This suburb had its own church, which was dedicated to St Clement – a saint associated with areas of Danish settlement. The medieval church was demolished in 1829/30, leaving an open space known as 'The Plain' at the junction of St Clement's Street and the Iffley and Cowley roads. The photograph shows The Plain around 1920 and in 2013. *Previous Page:* Victorian terraces in the Iffley Road.

The Boer War Memorial

Oxford's Boer War memorial, commemorating 142 members of the Oxfordshire Light Infantry who had died in South Africa, was unveiled in the old churchyard on The Plain on 19 September 1903. The monument initially comprised four bronze tablets upon a Portland stone plinth, but a 7-foot bronze figure of a soldier was subsequently added, and in 1906 *The Oxfordshire Light Infantry Chronicle* reported that this additional work had been 'entrusted to Messrs Boulton & Sons, sculptors of Cheltenham, the artist being Mr J. Hyatt, a constant exhibitor at the Royal Academy; while the casting was carried out by Messrs Singer of Frome'.

The memorial was removed in the 1950s and, as shown in the upper picture, its site is now occupied by a roundabout. The lower photograph shows the memorial shortly after its completion in 1906; it is now at Edward Brookes Barracks, near Abingdon.

St Clement's Church

The present St Clement's church, in Marston Road, was designed by Daniel Robertson and consecrated on 14 June 1828. The site was donated by Sir Joseph Locke, and the church, which consists of a nave, side-aisles and west tower, was paid for by public subscription. The upper view shows the church during the early years of the twentieth century, while the colour view was taken in 2013. Although the building is supposedly a 'Norman-style' structure, its symmetrical appearance reflects Georgian ideas of 'taste'. *Inset*: A detailed view of the tower.

St Clement's Street

St Clement's Street is one of three busy thoroughfares that radiate from The Plain, the other two being Cowley Road and Iffley Road. These two recent views are both looking east towards Headington, the lower photograph having been taken from a position slightly further to the east. The brick building with the tall gable was St Clement's Mission Hall, while the former Victoria Café can be seen to its right, on the corner of St Clement's and Boulter Street.

St Clements: The Victoria Café

This Edwardian postcard view provides a more detailed glimpse of the Victoria Café. This distinctive building was erected around 1886 and was, for a period of over thirty years, run as a café and boarding house by Walter Hazel and his wife Emma, who offered 'well-aired beds' and 'good and reasonable accommodation for cyclists and commercials'. Mr Hazel died in 1938, his wife having predeceased him by just six months; thereafter, the building was used for a time as an annexe to the neighbouring Mission Hall, though it subsequently became a 'Gospel Book Depot'; it is now the St Andrew's Christian Bookshop, as shown in the recent colour photograph.

Marston Street

Marston Street is one of many side streets in the St Clement's area. It forms a link between the Cowley and Iffley roads, and was first developed during the 1850s. The street contains a variety of different buildings, including two-storey terraced houses and a number of somewhat larger villas, as can be seen in the accompanying photographs. The upper view dates from around 1912, while the colour photograph was taken a century later in 2013.

St John the Evangelist Church

The church of St John the Evangelist in Iffley Road was built as a chapel for the Society of St John the Evangelist, an Anglican religious order that had been founded by Richard Meux Benson (1824–1915), Vicar of Cowley, in 1865. This impressive Victorian church was completed in 1896, the architect being Thomas Bodley (1827–1907), although the west tower was not added until 1902. The church is now part of an Anglican theological college known as St Stephen's House.

The upper photograph provides a general view of the church from the north-east, and was probably taken shortly after the completion of the tower. The colour view is a detailed study of the west tower, which features three tall buttresses – the massive centre buttress is adorned with a small relief carving of the Crucifixion. *Inset*: A detailed view of the Crucifixion; the female figures on either side represent St Mary and St John the Evangelist.

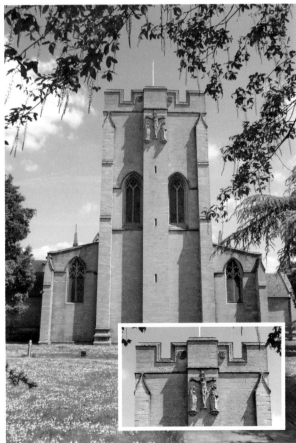

Divinity Road

Above: Running from north-east to south-west, Divinity Road was laid out by The Oxford Industrial & Provident Land & Building Society in 1891. When first erected, these neat, brick-built villas would typically have been occupied by bank clerks, shopkeepers, small businessmen and other lower middle-class residents. *Below*: A recent view, taken in 2013; the gas lamps have been replaced by electric lights, while the iron railings in front of the neat, brick-built houses were taken away for scrap during the Second World War.

Cowley Road Wesleyan Chapel

Designed by Stephen Salter, the Cowley Road Methodist chapel was built by Messrs Kingerlee & Sons of Oxford, and opened in 1904. It was able to seat 700 worshippers, while the adjacent school could accommodate 500 pupils. With its curious turrets and boldly-curved buttresses the building is unexpectedly flamboyant for a Nonconformist chapel; the upper view shows building shortly after its completion, while the colour photograph was taken in June 2013.

The University & City Arms

Above: This somewhat forbidding Victorian pub was situated on the corner of Cowley Road and Magdalen Road, in convenient proximity to the Cowley Road tramway terminus. The landlord in 1895 was William King. *Below*: The building was demolished by Messrs Ind Coope around 1937 and, in its place, the brewery firm built a slightly larger pub with three bars. In 1995, the pub was renamed The Philosopher & Firkin by Allied Domecq, but it is now known as the City Arms.

Bedford Street

Bedford Street is one of a number of side streets in a residential area to the west of the Iffley Road and, like Marston Street and Divinity Road, it was intended to provide for the needs of Victorian lower-middle-class households. The upper view, from a postcard of *c.* 1912, is looking westwards, while the colour photograph, taken in June 2013, is looking east towards Warwick Street. These nineteenth-century villas are only a short distance away from the River Thames.

The Melville Hotel

Nos 214–218 Iffley Road, formerly The Melville Hotel, are now used as student accommodation. At first glance, these substantial Victorian buildings seem to have an affinity with the nineteenth-century villas in North Oxford, although they are in an urban setting beside a busy main road, rather than an exclusive suburb. Advertisements reveal that, in the mid-1930s, the Melville Hotel had thirteen double or twin rooms; bed and breakfast was available 'from 7s 6d', while the cost of an evening meal was 3s 6d.

St Hilda's College

St Hilda's College was founded in 1893 by Dorothea Beale (1831–1906), the Principal of Cheltenham Ladies' College. Men have been admitted since 2008, but St Hilda's was, until that time, an exclusively female establishment. The college, which is sited in attractive surroundings beside the River Cherwell, boasts a diverse range of buildings, some of which pre-date the college, while others were added in the nineteenth and twentieth centuries.

The upper picture shows the main gateway to the college; the lodge was built as recently as the 1950s, although parts of the 'Hall Building' behind it date back to the 1780s. The lower view provides a glimpse of the college from the riverbank. The Victorian Gothic building visible in the distance is Cherwell Hall, which was originally a private house, and later became a teachers' training college; the property was acquired by St Hilda's in 1902, and it is now known as 'The South Building'.

St Hilda's College

Above: This Edwardian postcard view shows Cherwell Hall, which was designed by William Wilkinson and erected in 1878. *Below*: The present 'Hall Building' was built around 1780 as a private house for Dr Humphrey Sibthorp (1713–97), Sherardian Professor of Botany. It subsequently became the home of his son, John Sibthorp (1758–96), the celebrated botanist and author of *Flora Oxoniensis*, a guide to the plants of Oxfordshire. Sibthorpe's main work, *Flora Graeca*, was published many years after his death.

St James's Church, Cowley

Although now regarded as a sprawling outer suburb of Oxford, Cowley originally comprised the villages of Temple Cowley and Church Cowley. The church of St James, in Church Cowley, was rebuilt by G. E. Street during the 1860s, the most significant modification carried out at that time being the addition of a much-enlarged nave, which now dwarfs the rather stubby west tower. The upper view shows the interior of the church around 1912, while the colour photograph was taken in June 2013.

Cowley Barracks

Cowley Barracks was built in connection with the Cardwell reforms, which were initiated between 1869 and 1871 by Edward Cardwell (1813–86), the Secretary of State for War. It was decided that a network of regional military 'depots' would be established, and in 1873 *The Times* reported that the War Office purchased 20 acres of land in what was then open countryside, about 2 miles south-east of Oxford. Despite protests from Oxford University, construction of the barracks proceeded apace between 1874 and 1876, most of the building work being carried out by Messrs Downs & Co. of Southwark at a contract price of £45,000. The depot was opened on 7 June 1876, and the the first units to occupy the site were the 52nd (Oxfordshire) Light Infantry and the 85th (Bucks Volunteers) Regiment. The upper view shows the Barracks around 1912, while the lower photograph was taken during an 'Open Day' in 1938.

Cowley Barracks: The Keep

Above: The most obvious feature of the barracks was a tall, castle-like building known as 'The Keep'. This distinctive structure incorporated four full stories, together with two somewhat taller stair towers at the north-western and south-eastern corners of the building. The medieval theme was further underlined by the provision of crenellations around the parapet of the main block and on top of the towers, the latter being boldly machicolated. *Below*: A sketch plan showing the layout of Cowley barracks.

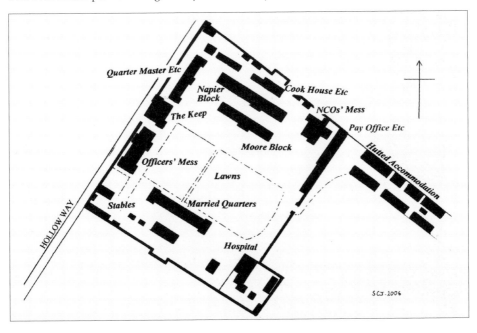

Cowley Barracks: Moore Block

The barracks contained a range of accommodation, including offices, mess rooms, an armoury, stores, married quarters, a guardroom, cook-house and stables, as well as a hospital. There were, in addition, two typical Victorian barrack blocks for the rank-and-file, and these were known as Moore Block and Napier Block. The upper view shows Moore Block in 1926 during a 'Pageant of Time' military tattoo, while the lower photograph shows Napier Block in 2007.

Cowley Barracks: Napier Block
Above: A presentation parade in progress outside Moore Block on 14 June 1930. *Below*: The facilities at Cowley were run down during the 1960s, the two barrack blocks being sold to GPO Telephones in 1965 – although the Officers' Mess remained in use as a Royal Green Jackets regimental office until 1968. The keep was, unfortunately, demolished, but Napier Block is still extant, as shown in this 2007 colour view. The neighbouring officers' mess building is now part of Oxford Brookes University.

The Oxfordshire & Buckinghamshire Light Infantry Memorial

Towards the end of 1920, it was decided that the 5,878 members of the the Oxfordshire & Buckinghamshire Light Infantry who had lost their lives in the First World War would be commemorated by a Regimental war memorial. The architect Sir Edward Lutyens (1869–1944) was commissioned to design the memorial, which was in the form of a Portland stone obelisk, some 29 feet in height. It was hoped that the new memorial would be sited in convenient proximity to Cowley barracks but, in the event, problems with land acquisition meant that the obelisk, which was unveiled on 11 November 1923, was placed in what was then 'the corner of an orchard at the junction of the Henley and Cowley roads as they enter Oxford from the east'. The upper view shows the memorial surrounded by open countryside in 1923, whereas the recent photograph reveals that the area has now been thoroughly suburbanised. *Inset*: The cap badge of the Oxfordshire & Buckinghamshire Light Infantry.

Cowley Barracks: Soldiers' Cottage Homes

These two cottages, which were paid for by public subscription, were erected in Cowley High Street to accommodate disabled soldiers, and to commemorate those who had died in the Boer War. The first occupants were Private W. Tripp, who lost his eyesight in South Africa, and Private J. Kearsley, who was severely wounded at Klip Kraal. One of the cottages is now used by a car valeting firm, while the other is the Cufa's Lea Veterinary Centre, as shown in the colour photograph.

MORRIS
leads again

YET again MORRIS leads at Olympia. For 1931 improved specifications, more comprehensive equipment, important price reductions and a wider range of models, further consolidate the proud position of leadership in value which MORRIS cars have held so consistently in the past.

MORRIS value cannot be measured by low first cost alone. Sound design, comfort, economy, reliability, performance, complete equipment, quality of material and workmanship, low depreciation and country-wide service facilities, all contribute to making MORRIS value unapproachable. You can make no safer purchase.

STAND 108

Write for New Catalogue to Enquiries Dept. "T" Cowley

MORRIS MAJOR SIX

A new light six-cylinder 15 h.p. model with a sparkling road performance. Equipment includes air cleaner and frame con-turning engine head, automatic radiator shutters, oil cleaner, grouped chassis oiling, powerful four-wheel brakes and full body equipment. Fabric Sports Salonette illustrated £215.

CHROMIUM FINISH AND TRIPLEX GLASS STANDARD

Four-cylinder models from £125.

Motor Houses from £9 15s. carriage paid. Deferred terms arranged.

MORRIS-COWLEY

The 11.9 h.p. Morris-Cowley for 1931 possesses greater engine power and is fitted with improved brakes, Bishop finger-light cam-type steering, grouped chassis oiling and a larger radiator and scuttle, which together with new body lines give a greatly enhanced appearance. Saloon £185.

BUY BRITISH AND ⚘ BE PROUD OF IT

William Morris & the Origins of Cowley Works

Born in Worcester, the eldest son of Frederick Morris of Witney and his wife Emily, William Morris (1877–1963) attended Cowley village school until the age of fifteen, and having been apprenticed for a short time to an Oxford bicycle-maker, he set-up his own business at the age of just sixteen. The new venture prospered, and in 1913 Morris produced his first motor car – the 2-seater Morris Oxford. In 1912, Morris rented a former school at Cowley known as the Military College, which he adapted for use as a car factory. An additional building, known as the Old Tin Shed, was built to the north of the school, while 'B-Block' and the main production lines were added in the 1920s and 1930s respectively; by 1939, the car plant employed over 2,000 people. The upper view shows car engines being assembled, while the lower illustration shows a Morris advertisement from 1931.

A full range of 1927 Morris models is available for inspection at ease and leisure at the Acton and New Bond Street Depots of our London Distributors, Messrs. Stewart & Arden, Ltd.

PRICES FROM £148 10s.

Prospective Purchasers from Overseas should communicate direct with our Export Department at Cowley.

The new 15.9 h.p. Morris-Oxford is shown in Chassis form at Olympia. A complete five-seater is available for inspection at Acton.

The New Morris-Cowley Saloon, £195.

Morris Motors & the Pressed Steel

Above: A further Morris advertisement, from around 1927, depicting 'the new Morris-Cowley saloon', which was reasonably priced at just £195. *Below*: Engines being tested in the Morris factory at Cowley. By 1930, Morris Motors had overtaken Ford as Britain's largest car manufacturer. William Morris was awarded a baronetcy in 1929, and in 1938 he became Viscount Nuffield. In addition to his role as an industrialist, Morris was also a noted philanthropist, who donated more than £30,000,000 to charitable causes.

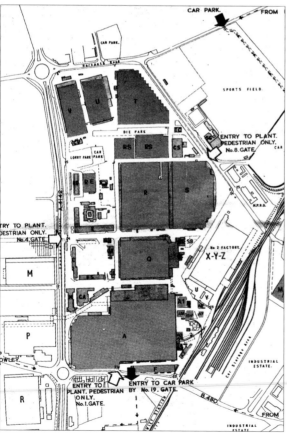

Morris Motors & the Pressed Steel

In 1926, Morris had opened the Pressed Steel body plant at Cowley as a new joint venture with the Budd Company of America and J. Henry Schroder, a merchant bank. Morris and the Budd Company subsequently withdrew, leaving Pressed Steel as an independent concern; there were thus two factories at Cowley, although both eventually became part of the British Motor Corporation (later British Leyland).

After many vicissitudes, the Cowley factories were acquired by BMW. The North and South Morris works were demolished, but the former Pressed Steel site was modernised and re-equipped so that it could produce an all-new version of the highly successful MINI. The upper view shows the part of the MINI plant in 2013, while the accompanying plan shows the layout of the Pressed Steel site in 1976, by which time it had become the Cowley Body Plant. Over 20,000 people worked at Cowley in the 1970s, whereas today's workforce is around 3,700.

CHAPTER 4

Oxford Villages

Beckley: Old Cottages in High Street & Otmoor Lane

Situated on high land to the north-east of Oxford, Beckley is a Cotswold-style village in well-wooded surroundings. Beckley was one of the 'seven towns of Otmoor' and, prior to enclosure in the early nineteenth century, the villagers had the right to graze their cattle, sheep and geese on the nearby moor. These two views are looking eastwards along the High Street towards Otmoor Lane. The upper view is an Edwardian colour-tinted postcard, whereas the lower photograph was taken in May 2013.

Beckley: High Street & the Abingdon Arms

The recent photograph was taken in May 2013, while the sepia postcard probably dates from around 1950; both of these views are looking westwards along the High Street, with the Abingdon Arms pub featuring prominently to the right. It is interesting to note that Beckley High Street appeared, albeit briefly, in an episode of the popular ITV detective series *Midsomer Murders* entitled 'Electric Vendetta'.

Beckley Church

The church of the Assumption of the Blessed Virgin Mary incorporates some Transitional Norman fabric, although the present building dates mainly from the Decorated period. It consists of a short nave flanked by north and south aisles, together with a central tower, chancel and south porch. The building was remodelled in the fifteenth century, when the clerestory was added above the nave. The sepia postcard view probably dates from the 1930s, while the colour photograph was taken in May 2013.

Cumnor: Old Houses in the High Street

Cumnor, about 2½ miles to the south-east of Oxford, was transferred from Berkshire to Oxfordshire in 1974. The village retains a pleasant, rural atmosphere, as exemplified by this *c.* 1930 postcard, which is looking westwards along the High Street. The colour photograph, taken in May 2013, provides a more detailed view of No. 2 High Street, known as Manor Farmhouse – an L-shaped structure dating from the eighteenth century that probably contains remnants of a much earlier building.

Amy Robsart & Cumnor Place

Cumnor will always be associated with Amy Robsart, who moved to the village in 1559 and was found dead on 8 September 1560, having apparently fallen down the main stairway in Cumnor Place. The Berkshire Coroner decided that she had died *per infortunam* (by misfortune), but malicious rumours persisted to the effect that she had been murdered by her husband Robert Dudley, the favourite of Elizabeth I, so that he would be free to marry the Queen.

The upper view is a Victorian sketch of *c.* 1850, which must have been copied from an earlier print, because Cumnor Place was demolished in 1811. This medieval building had formerly belonged to the Abbot of Abingdon, but at the time of the tragedy the property was leased to Anthony Foster, who later became Keeper of Dudley's Wardrobe. The site of the mansion, immediately to the west of the church, is now occupied by an extension of the graveyard, as shown left.

Cumnor Church

St Michael's church, originally Transitional Norman, was rebuilt in the thirteenth and fourteenth centuries. In its present form, the building consists of a nave, north aisle, chancel and north porch, together with a transeptal chapel on the south side. The sepia view shows the church from the south-west, while the colour photograph was taken from the south-east in 2013. The south transept, which was added during the early fourteenth century, gives the exterior of the building a slightly unbalanced appearance.

Forest Hill: The Main Street

Like Beckley, Forest Hill is a hilltop village in well-wooded surroundings to the east of Oxford. The sepia postcard view shows part of Main Street, probably around 1912, while the colour photograph was taken from approximately the same position in May 2013. A number of properties have been demolished, but Merrick Cottage, which can be seen on the extreme right of the old view, is still extant. It is of stone construction with a thatched roof, and dates from the seventeenth century.

Forest Hill: The Church of St Nicholas

Dating mainly from *c.* 1200, the parish church consists of a nave, chancel and south porch, together with a Victorian north aisle that was added by G. E. Street in 1852. The west wall boasts a double bell-cote, and in 1639 two massive buttresses were built to support it. The lower view is a distant view from an adjacent field, whereas the recent photograph, taken in 2013, shows the heavily-buttressed west end of the building. John Milton was married to Mary Powell in this church in June 1642.

Godstow Nunnery & Fair Rosamund

Godstow, on the west bank of the Thames, about 4 miles north-north-east of central Oxford, is famous in connection with Rosamund Clifford (*c.* 1140–76), a mistress of Henry II, who was buried in a magnificent tomb near the High Altar of Godstow following her death at the age of around thirty-five. The nunnery became a private house after the Reformation, but most of it was destroyed during the Civil War. The upper view shows the ruined nunnery around 1910, while the colour photograph below was taken in 2013.

The Trout Inn, Godstow

The Trout Inn is said to have originated as an outbuilding of the nearby nunnery, although the present building dates mainly from the seventeenth century. In recent years, this famous riverside pub has featured prominently in Colin Dexter's 'Inspector Morse' novels and, as such, has appeared in several episodes of the popular television series. The sepia postcard probably dates from around 1925, whereas the colour picture was taken in 2013.

New Hinksey Vicarage & Church

Hinksey, formerly in Berkshire, consists of the villages of North Hinksey and South Hinksey, plus the Victorian suburb of New Hinksey. The upper view is an Edwardian postcard showing New Hinksey Vicarage and church, and the colour photograph was taken from a similar position in 2013. The expanse of water that can be seen in the foreground is a former ballast pit that was excavated during the construction of the railway; it later became a reservoir, and is now known as Hinksey Lake.

Horspath: Church Road

Horspath, just 1 mile to the east of Oxford's Eastern Bypass, is only a short distance from the industrial environs of Cowley. The 1932 edition of F. G. Brabant's *The Little Guide to Oxfordshire* warned that the village was 'fast becoming suburban', but in the event Horspath has remained a traditional rural village. The upper photograph is looking north-eastwards along Church Road towards the village school around 1920, while the colour photograph was taken from a position slightly further to the south in 2013. *Inset*: A detailed view of Horspath school, *c.* 1912.

Iffley from the River

Although it is now part of Oxford, Iffley has, like Horspath, retained an idyllic rural character. The ancient village is situated upon a low hillock beside the River Thames, around 2 miles to the south of Oxford city centre. The upper view shows Iffley church and rectory from the river, *c.* 1912, while the recent picture provides a detailed glimpse of Iffley Lock. Dating from around 1630, this was one of the first pound locks on the Thames, although the present lock was built in 1924.

Iffley: St Mary's Church

Iffley parish church is generally considered to be one of the finest Norman churches in England. It was probably built between 1170 and 1180, and retains its original 'axial' plan, with an aisle-less nave and chancel separated by a central tower. The upper view shows this interesting old church from the north, probably around 1912; the chancel is to the left, while the nave is to the right of the picture. The colour photograph, taken in June 2013, shows the south side of the building.

Iffley: The Church & Village

Left: This Edwardian postcard depicts the interior of St Mary's church, looking eastwards through the magnificently decorated Norman tower arches towards the chancel. The eastern bay of the chancel was rebuilt during the thirteenth century and some of the windows are later additions, but, otherwise, the church is a near-perfect example of late-Norman architecture, with a wealth of beakheads, chevrons and other carvings. *Below*: A recent view, showing old buildings in Church Way. No. 122, to the left of the picture, was originally known as Court House, while the thatched building to the right is a former barn, which was adapted for use a Parochial School in 1838. In the meantime, a separate school had been established with the aid of a bequest from Sarah Nowell, and in 1853 the two schools were amalgamated. The school was closed in 1961, and the building has now found a new role as the church hall.

Iffley: Old Buildings in Church Way

Iffley's main street, known as Church Way, winds through the village from Iffley Turn to the famous church. These contrasting views are looking northwards along Church Way during the early years of the twentieth century, and in June 2013. No. 92, Rivermead, which can be seen in the centre of the sepia view, has an unusual gabled porch. Interestingly, some of these old houses have wells in their cellars, Church Way being built above a network of springs and streams.

Iffley: Mill Lane

Situated at the corner of Church Way and Mill Lane, No. 2 Mill Lane is a picturesque old thatched property that was probably built during the early seventeenth century. The upper view dates from the early years of the twentieth century, whereas the colour photograph was taken in June 2013.

The Tandem Inn, Kennington

Two Edwardian postcard views of Kennington which, like Iffley, has been absorbed into Oxford. The upper picture shows the River Thames at Kennington Island, while the old thatched building depicted in the lower view is a pub in Kennington Road that was, at one time, known as The Fish, although it was renamed The Tandem around 1915. This popular riverside pub still exists, but the present-day Tandem is very different, the building having been extensively rebuilt.

Wolvercote Canal Junction

Wolvercote, about 4 miles to the north of Oxford town centre, and now joined to the city by ribbon development, is both a canal junction and a railway junction. The upper picture shows the canal junction in 2013, while the lower view provides a glimpse of the narrowboat *Pearl* moored at the same location around 1967. It is believed that *Pearl* was built at Braunston as an unpowered 'butty' for Thomas Claytons Ltd in 1935, and rebuilt as a motor boat in 1945.

Holy Rood Church, Woodeaton

The tiny, Cotswold-style village of Woodeaton is situated some 6 miles to the north-east of Oxford. Holy Rood church, which dates mainly from the thirteenth century, consists of a nave, chancel and tower, the tower being a later addition that is supported upon massive piers at the west end of the nave. The upper view shows the church in 2013, while the sepia postcard provides a glimpse of the Old Rectory, probably around 1930.

Wytham Abbey & All Saints Church

Wytham is another Cotswold-style village, with stone-built houses and cottages. It nestles beneath the magnificently-wooded Wytham Hills, and is only a short distance from the River Thames. Prior to local government reorganisation in 1974, it had been the most northerly village in Berkshire, but it is now part of Oxfordshire.

The upper picture shows the manor house, which is known as Wytham Abbey, although there is no evidence that it was ever used as an abbey or religious house. The building, once the seat of the Earls of Abingdon, has now been divided up into private apartments. The lower illustration shows All Saints church, a fourteenth- and fifteenth-century building that was rebuilt around 1812, using architectural fragments from Amy Robsart's house at Cumnor (*see page 76*). The medieval gateways that can be seen in the picture were both taken from Cumnor Place; the one on the left is dated 1372.

Wytham: Colonel ffennell's Generosity

In 1920, the Wytham estate was purchased by the philanthropist Colonel Raymond ffennell (1871–1944), who allowed Wytham Woods to be used for educational purposes by inner-city children. Prior to his death, Colonel ffennell made arrangements for the 3,108 acre estate to be transferred to Oxford University by gift, sale and bequest, the conditions upon which the sale and gift were made being designed to preserve the character of the estate in perpetuity. The accompanying pictures show the village pub around 1906, and in 2013.

Wytham: The Village Street

These 'then and now' views are both looking westwards along the main street. The upper photograph dates from the early years of the twentieth century, and the recent view, which shows two of the old cottages in greater detail, was taken in June 2013. Writing in 1911, Frederick Brabant said that Wytham was 'highly-picturesque, consisting of well-built stone cottages lying amongst well-kept garden, where strawberries are largely grown'. He added that, at the end of June, 'all Oxford comes here to eat strawberries'.

Wytham: Old Cottages in Botley Road

The two photographs show traditional stone cottages in Botley Road, the upper view dating from around 1913, while the lower view was taken a century later in June 2013. The cottage in the foreground has clearly been modernised, but the neighbouring L-shaped house appears to be in more or less its original condition.

Around Oxford: Envoi

Two final views of Oxford villages and suburbs in the summer of 2013. The upper picture shows the lower end of Bedford Street, with Thames-side meadows visible just beyond the Victorian terraced houses. The lower view depicts part of St Andrew's Road in Old Headington. The houses that can be seen in the picture are clearly of no great antiquity but, with the church in the background, they form part of a pleasant village scene.